TEACHING
A LIVING
LANGUAGE

TEACHING
A LIVING
LANGUAGE

Ralph M. Hester, Editor
STANFORD UNIVERSITY

CONTRIBUTORS

Karl C. Diller
HARVARD UNIVERSITY

Ralph M. Hester
STANFORD UNIVERSITY

Yvone Lenard
CALIFORNIA STATE COLLEGE
DOMINGUEZ HILLS

Pierrette Spetz
CLAYTON VALLEY HIGH SCHOOL
CONCORD, CALIFORNIA

◇

HARPER & ROW, PUBLISHERS
New York, Evanston, and London

TEACHING A LIVING LANGUAGE

LIBRARY OF CONGRESS CATALOG CARD NUMBER: 79-116833

CONTENTS

PREFACE

Even in order to understand we have to invent, or, that is, to reinvent, because we can't start from the beginning again. But I would say that anything is only understood to the extent that it is reinvented.

JEAN PIAGET

Audio-lingual "New Key" methods have long been held suspect, because the millennial results expected were not produced. Some teachers protested early, others waited only a few years. In January, 1968, a *Newsweek* magazine article drew national attention to the deplorably incompetent American student of foreign language as reported by John Carroll's research team and released by the U.S. Office of Education in 1967. Since then a wave of negative criticism—previously an undercurrent beneath the vogue of structuralist theory—has been pounding against language teaching methodology as practiced during the last decade. Present misgivings about language teaching often concern the relatively rigid sequence prescribed by most variants of the audio-lingual method. Unfortunately, it is denounced not only for its inherently rigid dullness, but for its anti-intellectualism as well. Unfortunate, because now almost any method with an oral goal is taken to be anti-intellectual, and the wrath of many university foreign language and literature departments is being addressed to the secondary schools. Professors despair about "oral-aural" teaching—a term used twenty and thirty years ago—as if it were synonymous with "audio-lingual."

This curiously negative attitude towards speaking a language is by no means shared by all intellectuals. I. A. Richards, for one, considers learning either to read or to speak a foreign language like writing a poem:". . . the resemblance to the process above sketched of the composition of a poem is, at least, suggestive. And so is the resemblance to the process of learning to read or to speak a second language encouraged by a self-critical theory of the design of instruction, where the student is invited to explore an intelligible sequence of oppositions and connections rather than to memorize what he hopes teacher would like to hear from him."[1] Needless to say, Richards is not the only humanist to have such an opinion. Rabelais' Panurge spoke twelve languages and, indeed, "invented" one more, which he spoke as well.

Having to defend the speaking of language seems to mark a regression toward the polarized attitudes of another age. Yet we are hearing cries of "humanism" as opposed to the "utilitarianism" of speaking another tongue. The current polemics of "literature" versus "language" place both teachers of language and literature in a most disadvantageous position to combat the clear post-Sputnik trend away from foreign languages. Many of our major universities and colleges no longer have an admission or B.A. language requirement. In December, 1968, foreign language department chairmen from across the nation met to consider "The Threat to the Language Requirement." Everywhere, we see a tendency to abandon foreign language, among various other disciplines, because they are a hindrance to the young learner's freedom, self-discovery, and natural "creativity." Be that as it may, foreign language should not be discarded as an obstruction to creativity, for in spite of the uncreative way in which languages have been taught for the last decade or so, nothing is more creative than language learning; and "creative" in the sense that estheticians, teachers of literature, and educational psychologists use the word is not incompatible with the connotations that generative grammarians give to it. Language can be "invented," and this inventiveness, so stifled by the usual audio-lingual methods, is quite opposed to procedures of mimicry and memorization, which have become so widely practiced.

For some time now Carroll and others have been declaring the need for rethinking the whole problem of language teaching. Those of us contributing to this collection of essays have been doing exactly that, and we hasten to point out that our theoretical conclusions—obviously still open to elaboration or rejection—remain supported by our language teaching experiences. While discussing the possibility of a methodology in harmony with the human mind's creative ability in language, we do not claim to offer a series of irrefutable proofs. We do offer our essays as a record of reflection and experience. Perhaps we should have waited a dozen years for the compilation of great numbers of experiments. In any case, we commit no greater transgression than that of the audio-lingual purveyors now more and more impatient to admit the lack of experimental evidence. "Up to the present," Nelson Brooks has recognized, "what is called the new approach is largely an act of faith; research to prove the validity of its basic principles is scanty."[2] We, on the contrary, are convinced we have gone a step beyond pure faith, because we are satisfied with the results, and, unlike the case of the New Key, we have found only the greatest enthusiasm among those using our method. We are, therefore, not so much arguing as showing what *can* be done. We know, of course, even more remains to be done. Penetrating the deep mystery of the language function of the mind is clearly yet to come. We have been convinced in the classroom of the extraordinary and unexploited inventive capacity of the young mind learning a foreign language, but we readily admit with Chomsky, that " . . . the central problems relating to the creative aspect of language use remain as inaccessible as they have always been."[3]

In the meantime, there is an alternative to audio-lingual methods without returning to the generally discredited traditional method of grammar-translation. A method which is creative, interesting, stimulating, definitely oral and definitely not anti-intellectual does, in fact, exist, and it is not a method to be seen as the pure opposite of audio-lingual. In some recent comparative experiments the term "code-cognitive" has been wrapped around certain essentially traditional methods and contrasted with results of "audio-lingual." This will be further discussed in a later chapter. The method we propose is a direct one, but not "direct" as it is usually understood. Ours is a rationalist direct method in which foreign language learning occurs at once systematically and yet with a wide margin of invention left to the student in the dynamic situation of the classroom. Instruction takes place only in the target language, yet grammar is methodically taught, gradually, step by step, in logical sequence to provide the tools of language creation. We simultaneously use all language skills: listening-understanding, spoken and written expression, and reading. This method derives from the well-known de Sauzé method, or Cleveland Plan, and, in particular, the variants of that method which have been elaborated and experimented on in the last several years.

One of the distinctive ways our method differs from much current practice is in its emphasis on original composition and in its reversal of the usual reading-writing order. We teach composition in the foreign language before approaching the study of serious reading. Such a procedure is only to the advantage of the reader's eventual skill and, ultimately, to his greater appreciation of literature. He who is able to create is able to appreciate the creation of another. This was one of the conclusions of the international conference on the teaching of literature at Cerisy-la-Salle in the summer of 1969. Roland Barthes, for one, suggested that if he were a French lycée teacher of literature, he would attempt first of all to enable students to accede to a real participation in writing, to make them participate in what he called the experience of language, and he even went so far as to say that, ideally, young readers should be transformed from receivers of texts into producers of texts.[4]

Creativity in writing as a means to the reading of literature is, of course, but one aspect of our method. In many ways it may appear to some quite "traditional." To the extent that it has grown out of the de Sauzé method, however, we would point out that the Cleveland Plan was never "traditional," even though very old. It was never widely used on a national scale. In fact, at present it appears very new, because the small but increasing number of foreign language textbooks derived from the Cleveland Plan are only now finding their theoretical justification in the studies of Chomsky and other linguists who have largely rejected the behaviorist concept of language held by structural descriptive linguists. The implications of the "Chomsky revolution," as Lado and other linguists call it, are paralleled and complemented on the practical level already by some most promising classroom results. The method of de Sauzé's *Cours pratique de Français pour commençants* (1919) was not seriously modified or extended until Yvone Lenard's *Parole et Pensée* (1965). Since 1965, Vincenzo Traversa's *Parola e Pensiero*, Franz Pfister's *Deutsch durch Deutsch*, Pucciani and Hamel's *Langue et Langage*, John Barson's *La Grammaire à l'Oeuvre*, and Mrs. Lenard's secondary-level adaptation, *Jeunes Voix, Jeunes Visages*, have appeared.

Mrs. Lenard discusses her method in the second chapter of this book. What she calls the "verbal-active" method is, indeed, what we understand by a rationalist direct method. Since Pierrette Spetz and I have both used Mrs. Lenard's texts, most of our examples are in French. Had our competence and experience been with the Italian or German texts inspired by *Parole et Pensée*, our examples could just as well have been in those languages. We are happy to include in these pages the essay by Mrs. Spetz, a high school teacher, whose long experience and success in teaching foreign languages at the secondary level have given a voice of pragmatic authenticity to our undertaking. The link is clear between her practical remarks and the theories of language acquisition discussed in the first chapter by our colleague in linguistics, Karl Diller. We had at one time considered inviting a student to collaborate with us, but some student comment will be found in my own chapter on direct method experiences at university levels. These essays will thus show not only how the most recent linguistic theory proposes a view of language and language learning quite different from that of structural linguistics, but also how such theory has already been successfully put into practice at both university and pre-college levels.

Unlike our method, this book will undoubtedly bear the mark of its time. The current situation in language teaching is not what it was five years ago. Theoretical linguistics is in a period of agitation and transition. Foreign language teaching is, likewise, already in a period of agitation, but not yet of transition. We hope it soon will be.

R. M. H.

Tours
September, 1969

Notes

1. I. A. Richards, "The Secret of 'Feedforward,'" *Saturday Review*, Feb. 3, 1968, p. 16.
2. Nelson Brooks, "Language Learning: The New Approach," *Phi Delta Kappan*, March, 1966, p. 359.
3. Noam Chomsky, *Language and Mind*, New York, Harcourt, Brace, & World, 1968, p. 84.
4. Roland Barthes, July 24, 1969, at the *Décade de Cerisy-la-Salle*. The discussions of the colloquium having not yet been published, the translation is based on approximate quotations from my own rough notes.

TEACHING
A LIVING
LANGUAGE

1

Karl C. Diller

LINGUISTIC THEORIES
OF LANGUAGE ACQUISITION[1]

A CENTURY ago, François Gouin went off to Hamburg to learn German. He had been a Latin teacher while a university student in France, and he thought that the quickest way to master German would be to memorize a German grammar book and a table of the 248 irregular German verbs. It took him only ten days of concentrated effort to do this in the isolation of his room. Then he decided to go out into the world, to the university, to see how much German he could understand. "But alas!" he writes, "in vain did I strain my ears; in vain my eye strove to interpret the slightest movements of the lips of the professor; in vain I passed from the first class room to a second; not a word, not a single word would penetrate to my understanding. Nay, more than this, I did not even distinguish a single one of the grammatical forms so newly studied; I did not recognize even a single one of the irregular verbs just freshly learnt, though they must certainly have fallen in crowds from the lips of the speaker."[2]

Gouin then decided that in order to really possess the foundations of the German language, he ought to memorize all the German roots. It took him only a week to do this— to memorize the 800 roots and to digest again the grammar book and 248 irregular verbs. But the result at the university was the same as before: he was unable to recognize a single word in the lecture hall. Furthermore, whenever, he tried to speak with townspeople, they would always laugh at his awkward attempts. Reading was no better—it took him a whole day to decipher and translate a single page from Goethe or Schiller.

At this point Gouin decided to try another method. He bought a textbook with basic sentences and dialogues for memorization, promising to teach German in ninety lessons. In three weeks he mastered the book; but he had not mastered the German language. The results were still the same as before. He was clearly not learning German in any useful way. German linguistics? Perhaps. But the ability to understand or to read German, no. What should he do?

"There still remained one last method," Gouin tells us, "but one so strange, so extraordinary, so unusual—I might say, so heroic—that I hardly dared propose it to myself. This supreme means was nothing else than to learn off the whole dictionary."[3] This he did. He learned 30,000 words in thirty days. Let us allow Gouin to tell us the results: "The third week gave me the third quarter of the dictionary; the thirtieth day I turned page 314, the last; and more triumphant than Caesar, I exclaimed, 'Vici!' That same evening I went to seek my crown at the university—a crown surely well merited. To comprehend what now happened to me it is necessary to have studied profoundly, as I have since been able to do, the question of language; to have determined accurately the conditions in which mankind, infant or adult, must be placed that they may be able to learn any language, no matter which. I understood not a word—not a single word! . . . And I permit no one to doubt the sincerity of this statement. 'Not a word—not one single word.' "[4]

His reading ability had improved slightly, but it still took him a day and a half to decipher two or three pages.

François Gouin had memorized the grammar, the irregular verbs, the roots, and the dictionary of German. He had memorized a textbook's basic sentences and dialogues. Why was he unable to understand or read the language? *It was because he treated German as a dead language.* Even when memorizing basic sentences and dialogues, German was still a dead language. As he said, "The word was always as a dead body stretched upon the paper. Its meaning shone not forth under my gaze; I could draw forth neither the idea nor the life. 'Tragen,' for instance, was for me but an arbitrary assemblage of six letters, perfectly incapable of revealing to me the effort or the special movement it had the mission to represent."[5]

Gouin's failure is not all that unusual. In 1965, 90 percent of the graduating French majors in American colleges failed to reach a level of "minimum professional proficiency" in speaking ability—a level only half way to "full bilingual proficiency." In reading ability, 50 percent were unable to do more than read non-technical news items or technical writing in a special field.[6] These are students who had been specializing in French for four years in college, and three-fourths of them had studied French in high school as well.

Why do America's French majors compare so unfavorably with native speakers of French? Is it impossible to master foreign languages in a reasonable amount of time? No, we all know of foreign students who perform marvelously in English (except perhaps for a harmless foreign accent). The task is far from impossible, yet it is evident that many of our efforts to teach and to learn foreign languages are wasted efforts.

To be effective in teaching languages, we must first understand what happens when a person really learns a language. How do *children* learn languages? Why are some situations more conducive to language learning than others are? What is a *language* in the first place? These are questions of linguistic theory; *the language teacher who understands what he is doing is by definition a linguistic theorist.*

Some language teachers try to avoid thinking through these basic questions for themselves, by accepting the authority of professional linguists. This is a dangerous attitude in any field, but it is especially dangerous in linguistic theory because there has never been general agreement on the questions of language acquisition. This has been a controversial matter throughout more than four centuries of the modern era, with analogues in the medieval and ancient worlds.

Most of the controversies have been centered on differences between *empiricist* and *rationalist* theories of language acquisition.[7] At present, an empiricist position is held by structural and descriptive linguists of the Bloomfield school. A rationalist position is held by generative grammarians, who, following Noam Chomsky, have brought about a radical transformation in linguistics since 1957.

Methods of language teaching are ways of carrying out the theoretical *approaches*, and the history of language teaching methodology is immensely simplified if we look for two separate developments of language teaching during the modern era: methods based on the empiricist approach and those based on the rationalist approach.

Briefly, the two approaches can be summed up as follows:

The basic *empiricist* position is that language acquisition is a kind of habit formation through conditioning and drill. Descriptive linguists affirm that the normal use of language is either mimicry or analogy; grammatical rules are merely descriptions of habits, and in normal fast speech, they say, a person has no time to apply rules as recipes for sentence formation. In its behaviorist extreme, as held by many descriptive linguists, the empiricist position holds that human beings use basically the same learning processes as other animals do—a stimulus-response model of conditioning. Leonard Bloomfield, the behaviorist father of twentieth-century American linguistics, maintained that vocal human language is not essentially different from gesture language or animal language.[8] Some people in the empiricist tradition have maintained that the mind is a "blank tablet" upon which the outside world imposes various sorts of knowledge; the behaviorists refuse to go so far as to talk of "knowledge" or of "mind"—for them the human being is essentially a machine with a collection of habits which have been molded by the outside world.

This approach has led to methods of mimicry, memorization, and pattern drill, advocated not only in the current audio-lingual method, but also in the "Army method" of World War II. In 1916, Harold E. Palmer published a book of pattern drills for English as a foreign language, and he recommended mimicry and memorization as well.[9] Even before this, in the late nineteenth century, various European linguists had advocated similar procedures in their "Reform method," or "Imitative method."[10]

On the other side, the *rationalist* position holds that man is born with the ability to think. He is equipped with a highly organized brain that permits certain kinds of mental activity that are impossible for other animals—for instance, man is the only animal that can learn human languages (and virtually all human beings learn at least one language). The rationalist notes that on an abstract level, all languages work in the same way—they all have words and sentences and sound systems and grammatical relations—and he attributes these universals of language to the structure of the brain. Just as birds inherit the ability to fly, and fish to swim, men inherit the ability to think and to use language in a manner which is unique to their species. A given language, English, for example, has to be learned, but the capacity to learn languages is inherited. The child is not a passive agent in language acquisition; he actively goes about learning the language of his environment. And what a person learns is more than a set of habits. If you read all the books in the English language, you will find very few sentences which are habitually used and are exact duplicates of each other—otherwise you would suspect quotation or plagiarism. Knowledge of a language allows a person to understand infinitely many new sentences, and to create grammatical sentences which no one else has ever pronounced but which will be understood at once by others who know the language.

Successful teachers in the rationalist tradition have included François Gouin (1831–1896) who invented the "Series Method" after his traumatic experience trying to learn German; Heness and Sauveur with their "natural method" (1875); M. D. Berlitz (1852–1921), founder of the Berlitz schools; and Emile B. de Sauzé (1878–1964), creator of the Cleveland Plan. Both Berlitz and de Sauzé used tightly organized "direct" methods similar to the one proposed in this book.

In this chapter we will make a fresh attempt to think through the issues involved in foreign language learning, and we will argue for a version of the rationalist approach. But if the teacher is to think independently for himself on the matter of language teaching, he will have to understand both the empiricist and the rationalist traditions of language teaching. In the process of studying them he will see how terribly important it is for the teacher to question the linguistic presuppositions of his teaching methods, since in his teaching he may well be trying to do something that is totally unrealistic. Linguistic theoreticians have frequently come up with impractical ideas about language teaching. But if the teacher is to develop practical methods for himself, he must understand what he is trying to do when he teaches a foreign language. The creative language teacher must be his own linguistic theoretician.

Let us turn, then, to a detailed examination of the two theoretical approaches to language learning, to see if we can gain a new understanding of the processes involved in foreign language acquisition.

THE EMPIRICIST APPROACH
TO LANGUAGE LEARNING

For the better part of a century linguists in the empiricist approach have agreed that foreign language teaching should consist of some combination of mimicry, memorization (or "mim-mem"), and pattern drill. Textbooks would first present a dialogue or a list of basic sentences with an English translation in parallel columns (see Table 1). Students have to be able to mimic these sentences perfectly, repeating them very quickly. Then these sentences are to be memorized so that the student can say them off rapidly when consulting only the English translation. After a sufficient amount of this rote activity, when the sentences are "overlearned," the student is put through pattern drills to produce a series of sentences which have the same structure as some of the memorized sentences (see Table 2). This kind of drill is also basically a rote activity; on a good pattern drill it is almost impossible for the student to make a mistake.

Table 1. A Dialogue for Memorization from an Intermediate Level Textbook for English as a Foreign Language[11]

SINGH: I brought my I. D. card to the Housing Office.

RAM: Why on earth did you go there?

SINGH: A couple of my books were missing. Somebody found them and took them there.

RAM: Were the people in the office very helpful?

SINGH: Yes. Speaking of books, there aren't any more economics texts on the shelves.

RAM: I know. I stood in line and bought one of the last copies. New.

SINGH: Yes. The cheap used copies went fast. But you can't save money that way.

RAM: Well, I'm applying for a student loan.

SINGH: A loan for next semester? Whose idea was that?

RAM: It came from the Foreign Student Advisor. I can repay some of the money with a summer job.

SINGH: What about right now? Are you short of cash?

RAM: No, thanks just the same. Next month there'll be a check in the mail from my government.

Table 2. Example of a Pattern Drill[12]

TEACHER	STUDENT I	CUE	STUDENT II
Are you going to the movies?	Are you going to the movies?	(zoo)	No, I'm going to the zoo.
__she__	Is she going to the movies?	(dance)	No, she's going to the dance.
__he__	Is he going to the movies?	(gym)	No, he's going to the gym.
__in the furniture business	Is he in the furniture business?	(mining)	No, he's in the mining business.
__they__	Are they in the furniture business?	(dry goods)	No, they're in the dry goods business.
__summer school	Are they in summer school?	(taking a vacation)	No, they're taking a vacation.

What are the reasons for this method? What is the theoretical approach which this method presupposes?

In popularizing their ideas about language learning, descriptive linguists have summed up their theory in a number of slogans, and the easiest way to grasp their theory is to examine their slogans. The best formulation of them is by William Moulton:[13] "Language is speech, not writing"; "A language is a set of habits"; "Teach the language, not about the language"; "A language is what its native speakers say, not what someone thinks they ought to say"; and "Languages are different."

Language Is Speech Not Writing

Language is not writing: the second half of the slogan is obvious enough. A large majority of the people who have lived in the world have never learned to read or write, yet almost all of them have learned a language. On the other hand, it is not so obvious that "language is speech." In fact, this claim is falsified by the single case history described by Lenneberg[14] of a boy who was physically unable to articulate a single speech sound. Yet this boy learned English, and understood it fully (he could take orders from a tape recorder), and he learned to read. For him, language was not speech.

Descriptive linguists have refused to admit that "knowledge" of a language might be primarily a matter of the mind, of mental activity. The "mind" could not be observed, so for purposes of science the descriptive linguists forced themselves to assume that "the mind does not exist."[15] The behavior of people talking is what we can observe, so the attempt was made to start with this speech behavior, analyze it and build up the grammar, going from sound to sentence. It was a "phonologically based grammar" or a building block (structural) grammar. First there were the *phonemes*, or distinctive sounds of the language. These sounds could be combined into meaningful units, *morphemes*. Then we make words out of morphemes (*blackberries* has three morphemes: *black, berry* and *s*). Finally we make sentences out of words. Sentences, then, are made up of concrete observable signs. If a sentence has no expressed subject (as in *Go home!*) then there is no subject at all (as opposed to the traditional grammarians who insisted that in this case the subject of *Go home!* is "*you* understood"). This slogan gives the reason for emphasizing the mimicry of sounds, the basic, crucial units of language.

A Language Is a Set of Habits

In trying to do away with "knowledge" and "mind," descriptive linguists assumed that a language was a set of (speech) habits, acquired by conditioning. Bloomfield described the child's acquisition of language in five steps: (1) First, the baby begins to babble—apparently because of an inherited trait. He eventually gains the habit of repeating a given mouth movement when he hears its corresponding sound. That is, he gains the ability to say *da-da-da* instead of just *da*. (2) Then when someone says *doll* in the baby's presence, the child hears *da* and repeats *da*. The child has begun to imitate. (3) The mother says *doll* so often in front of the baby's doll, that, in Bloomfield's words, "the child forms a new habit: the sight and feel of the doll suffice to make him say *da*." This is *classical conditioning*. (4) The habit of saying *da* when he sees his doll can be turned into abstract or displaced speech by a further process of classical conditioning. Suppose, Bloomfield suggests, that the child then gains the habit of saying *da* after his bath. But one day the mother forgets to give the baby the doll. When he says *da* this time, the mother interprets it as a question: the baby is asking for his doll. Thus the child begins to ask for things not present. (5) The child's speech is "perfected by its results" *(operant conditioning)*. The closer the baby's *da* is to the parents' *doll*, the more likely it will be that the parents bring the doll when it is asked for. Bad pronunciation will be extinguished by lack of the desired results.[16] This is Bloomfield's model for how a child could learn to speak without thinking.

The set of speech habits which one acquires by conditioning is thought to consist primarily of a set of basic sentences which a person has mimicked. New sentences can be built by analogy. As Hockett and others said, "whenever a person speaks, he is either mimicking or analogizing."[17] This is the whole basis for the methods of mim-mem and pattern drill. Memorization speeds up the process of establishing the basic treasury of sentences which can be extended by analogy; pattern drill provides the practice in making the analogies.

Teach the Language, Not About the Language

The slogan that we should teach the language, not about the language, is a warning to us not to teach a person the rules of the language. We are not to tell someone *how* to say things in the new language and then give him practice doing it. (Telling someone how to do something is the same as giving him a rule.) If for purposes of science we assume with the descriptivists that "mind does not exist," how can a "rule" have any reality? It can't. As Twaddell says, "a 'rule' of a language is the analytical statement of one of the habitual aspects of that language. We know that the habit is the reality and the rule is a mere summary of the habit."[18] To "teach the language" is to impose on the student a set of speech habits without assuming that he is capable of any (unobservable) mental activity. Building up speech habits in this way requires essentially rote methods. Mim-mem and pattern drill are well suited to this goal.

A Language Is What Its Native Speakers Say, Not What Someone Thinks They Ought to Say

This slogan furthers the attack on rules and goes against the whole concept of grammaticality. Students would be told "to 'copy what the native speaker says,' whether or not it agreed with what was in the textbook, because 'the native speaker is always right.' "[19] You can never make a mistake in your native language. A. A. Hill has even insisted that "Tall the man cigar the smoked black" could be a perfectly acceptable sentence in English, and, he says, "the fact that the meaning remains unknown is irrelevant."[20] But if deviations are acceptable in the speech of natives, the same tolerance is not extended to foreigners. Foreigners *can* make mistakes. Teachers in the empiricist approach have had a profound fear of mistakes, because mistakes are seen as the first step in forming bad habits. Pattern drills, therefore, have to be designed so that students will almost never make mistakes. With mimicry and memorization, of course, the danger of mistakes is almost nil. And the more memorization the better, for then a student will have a large stock of genuine sentences which a native speaker has already said.

Languages Are Different

The most important advice for a student of foreign languages, according to Bloomfield, is that languages are different. He begins his pamphlet on the practical study of foreign languages by telling the language learner to "start with a clean slate."[21] We are told to forget what we learned about language in school or college ("what little they teach is largely in error"), and above all, the student "must learn to ignore the features of any and all other languages, especially of one's own." The idea is that the most common cause of mistakes in a foreign language is interference from the native language. If someone suggests that an American who knows Spanish already will be able to learn French more quickly, it will be countered that related languages are especially misleading and that this person's French will show mistakes caused by two languages instead of by just one. As Martin Joos expressed it, "languages could differ from each other unpredictably and without limit."[22] There are no universal grammatical principles, and the student should not look for any; he should merely memorize the genuine utterances of native speakers and allow the habits of the language to be imposed upon him.

THE RATIONALIST APPROACH
TO LANGUAGE LEARNING

Since the late 1950s an increasingly large number of linguists have followed Noam Chomsky and other generative grammarians in rejecting the empiricist approach to language learning in favor of a sophisticated revival of the rationalist approach. This is the approach that underlies the Direct Method of M. D. Berlitz, and Emile B. de Sauzé's Cleveland Plan for the teaching of modern languages, as well as for the method of teaching a living language presented in this book. Let us organize our discussion around four propositions: (1) A living language is characterized by rule-governed creativity; (2) The rules of grammar are psychologically real; (3) Man is uniquely built to learn languages; (4) A living language is a language in which we can think.

A Living Language Is Characterized by Rule-Governed Creativity

"An intelligent adult is rarely successful in mastering a foreign language," says de Sauzé, "without learning in a functional way certain fundamental principles that govern the structure of that language and that enable him to generalize, to multiply his experience a thousand times. To know by memory even an ample stock of ready-made sentences in a language is not the same as to know that language."[23] Except for purposes of quotation, people rarely have occasion to use sentences that they have heard other people use. Take the first sentence to be memorized from Table 1: "I brought my I. D. card to the Housing Office." Have you ever been in a position to utter this sentence? To know a language is to be able to create *new* sentences in the language. In Chomsky's words, "normal linguistic behavior . . . is stimulus-free and innovative."[24] In most situations it is quite impossible to predict what will be said. The "stimulus" of this book, for example, will bring out different "responses" from every reader. Such stimuli obviously do not determine the responses.

But if language use is basically innovative, it is innovative only within the bounds of grammaticality. Not all collections of English words result in grammatical sentences. In fact, the chances are not great that you could find any six consecutive head words in a dictionary that would produce a grammatical sentence: "somnolent son sonance sonant sonar sonata."

It is the grammar that allows us to tell the difference between "The man led the horse too fast" and "The fast horse led the man, too." In a grammatical sentence we know what the subjects and predicates are. In the first sentence above, we know that the man did the leading and that "too" modifies "fast," making an adverbial phrase which tells us more about this particular act of leading. In the second sentence, the horse himself is fast and does the leading, and "too" modifies the whole sentence. Take the sentence quoted by Hill, above: "Tall the man cigar the smoked black." This sentence is clearly not grammatical. What is the subject? the predicate? What is the grammatical function of "black"? It is *not* irrelevant that the meaning remains unknown. In spite of the English words, this is not an English sentence.

The limitations of grammaticality rule out a large number of word combinations, but in spite of this the innovative power of language is theoretically infinite. There can be no limit to the length of sentences, and thus no limit to the number of different grammatical sentences. A given sentence can always be lengthened by absorbing other sentences into it. Many long parliamentary resolutions, with all their long "whereas" clauses, are no more than one sentence long—and we can always add another "whereas. . . ." But suppose we arbitrarily set a limit of twenty words for grammatical sentences. How many would we have then? George Miller has made a conservative estimate that there are at least 10^{20} grammatical twenty-word sentences in English. "Putting it differently," he says, "it would take 100,000,000,000 centuries (one thousand times the estimated age of the earth) to utter all the admissible twenty-word sentences of English. Thus the probability that you might have heard any particular twenty-word sentence before is negligible. Unless it is a cliché, every sentence must come to you as a novel combination of morphemes. Yet you can interpret it at once if you know the English language."[25]

This is to say that a rather small finite number of grammatical rules can produce an infinite number of sentences. A speaker does not have to store a large number of ready-made sentences in his head; he just needs the rules for creating and understanding these sentences.

In foreign language learning, understanding the fundamental rules of grammar can "multiply our experience a thousand times." That is to say that a conscious effort at figuring out how to say things will be rather more efficient than hoping that we will unconsciously learn how to say things if we memorize enough basic sentences. As de Sauzé puts it, "We found, also, in our experiment that the practical results, such as reading, writing, speaking, and understanding, were achieved in greater proportion and in less time when the technique involved a maximum amount of conscious reasoning."[26]

The Rules of Grammar Are Psychologically Real

Linguists are sometimes hesitant to say that ordinary people "know" the rules of their language, because linguists themselves have such a hard time trying to formulate these rules explicitly. Leonard Bloomfield, for example, seems to doubt whether unschooled people can isolate the different words of a sentence.[27] But words are obviously psychologically real units. When children learn to speak, the first thing they do is to isolate words. Only later do they combine them into sentences, and it is even later before they add the grammatical inflections and the articles *(a, an, the)*. A second piece of evidence is Pig Latin, a secret language that requires the speaker to know not only about words but about initial consonant clusters. Not only do children learn Pig Latin easily, they have no trouble "learning" that the sounds of a language are discrete elements which can be represented by the letters of the alphabet. Besides knowing about words and discrete sounds, children also know that the sounds are made up of distinctive features.[28] They may not be able to formulate this knowledge for you, but they know that the final sounds of *judge, church, bush, bus,* and *fez* form a natural class of strident consonants. Children know that the plural ending after strident consonants is pronounced [əz] (as in *buses*), and that after other sounds it is pronounced either [z] or [s] depending on whether those sounds are voiced or not (as in *cars, trucks*). Experiments have shown that this is a productive rule which children apply to nonsense words.[29] (If this is a *zug*, what are those?—They're *zugs*, too.)

But if children are not able to formulate the rules of grammar which they use, in what sense can we say that they "know" these rules? This is the question that has bothered linguists. The answer is that *they know the rules in a functional way, in a way which relates the changes in abstract grammatical structure to changes in meaning.* Knowledge does not always have to be formulated. Children can use tools before they learn the names for these tools.

The key distinction to note here is the difference between a rule and formulation of a rule. For example, Max Black has pointed out that there is a rule of chess to the effect that "A pawn on reaching the eighth rank must be exchanged for a piece." But there are other equally good formulations of this rule, among which Black lists these: "Pawns shall be promoted on reaching the end of the chessboard"; "Pawns reaching the last rank are replaced by pieces"; and "Pawns must be replaced by pieces whenever a further move would carry them off the chessboard." Further, as Black points out, "each of these formulations could be translated into German, or any other language containing names for chess pieces and their moves. . . . It follows from this that it would be a mistake to identify the rule about the promotion of pawns with any one of its formulations. For there is the one rule, but indefinitely many formulations of it."[30] Knowing a rule and being able to act on it is quite independent of being able to formulate the rule adequately. The rule can be psychologically real without any formulation of it.

It is worthwhile pursuing the matter of rule-following in chess, as it can help clear up some of the problems regarding rule-following in language. It is essential that chess be played according to the rules. If a player tries to move a rook diagonally across the chessboard (in *analogy* to the way bishops move), he is making an illegal move, and his opponent will surely stop him from this action. Legality in chess moves is like grammaticality in language. Just as we say "You can't do that in chess," we object to ungrammatical sentences with "You can't say it that way in English."

The chief argument given by the empiricists that language is a set of habits, not rules, is that language use is automatic and not on a level of intellectual awareness. As O'Connor and Twaddell put it, "There is no time for puzzle-solving or applications of rules in the real comprehension and use of a language. In real use the spoken words follow one another at the rate of several hundred a minute."[31] But in chess, after a little practice the application of rules becomes quite automatic. We do not think of the rules at all until our opponent tries to violate them. It is "analogy" that requires puzzle-solving; rules need only to be followed, not puzzled out.

The empiricist argument that language is learned by conditioning and drill also seems to rest entirely on the premise that language use is automatic. But this does not follow, either. The general fallacy involved is pointed out by Scheffler in discussing an argument of Ryle's. He says "What is it that leads Ryle to say that facilities are built up by drill? Surely his reason must be that facilities are routinizable, becoming increasingly automatic as they are developed. This does *not*, however, *at all* imply that drill alone is capable of building them up. Once they are developed, they are indeed automatic and repetitive; it cannot be inferred that they are therefore *acquired* in an automatic and repetitive way. . . . 'After the toddling-age,' says Ryle, 'we walk on pavements without minding our steps.' But then during the toddling-age we *do* mind our steps, and drill is, at least at this stage, inappropriate."[32] This should be an obvious point: routine and automatic facilities are often built up slowly and painstakingly. A good typist can type almost as easily as he speaks, without thinking about what he is doing; but when he first learned to type he had to spell out each word and concentrate on where to place each finger. The same is true of language learning. In de Sauzé's words, there are "two stages of knowledge of a language: the 'conscious' one, during which we use the language slowly, applying rules of grammar, reasoning various relationships as we proceed. The second one, . . . the 'automatic' stage, occurs when we speak, read, and write the language substantially like our mother tongue."[33]

What does it mean to "learn" the rules of grammar that we apply so carefully when we first speak a foreign language? It does *not* mean to memorize the formulations of the rules from a grammar book. Let us take again the example of chess: the most efficient way to master the rules of chess would not be to memorize the official rule booklet. Instead, one should have a teacher who would show him how to move each piece, how to castle, and how to capture the opponent's pieces. The teacher would help him make the moves and would guide him through his first game. Rules for action are best learned in conjunction with demonstration and practice of the action. The particular formulation of the rules is not terribly important: the rules of chess could probably be explained by sign language alone. But suppose that instead of explaining the rules you had a learner memorize some championship games: how much longer would it take for a person to figure out the simple moves that each piece can make! So it is with language. A few carefully chosen examples of a rule in operation can lead us to understand the rule. But embedding these examples in a dialogue to be memorized might mask their significance entirely.

Man Is Uniquely Built to Learn Languages

Perhaps the most striking phenomenon of language is its universality. Virtually every person in the world knows a language. Few other cultural phenomena are that universal. Equally noteworthy, perhaps, is the fact that lower animals cannot learn human language. A certain amount of communication is possible between man and animal, but it is not because the animals understand language. Try speaking to your dog in a foreign language—it will probably work as well as English. The universality of language learning would be a vacuous notion, of course, if it were true that "languages could differ from each other unpredictably and without limit."[34] But languages are not all that different, and, indeed, on an abstract level all human languages have a similar design. All languages have sentences made up of words. They can all produce arbitrarily long sentences by embedding sentences within other sentences. They all exhibit grammatical relationships such as subject and predicate. The words in all languages are made up of discrete sound segments, and these discrete sounds can be sorted into natural classes according to their distinctive features.[35] The similarities among all languages define human language as being qualitatively different from the so-called "animal languages," and they seem to be dependent on the biological make-up of man.

Human beings can overcome tremendous handicaps to learn languages. Blind children learn languages as easily as seeing children do. Deaf children can learn language through writing. Normal children of non-speaking deaf parents learn to speak with very little delay. We have already mentioned the child who was physically unable to articulate a single word and who learned, nevertheless, to understand English both in spoken and written form.[36] People with very defective intellects are not prevented from learning language—so long as a person reaches at least a mental age of six by the time he is twelve years old, he can and will learn a language. But in spite of persistent efforts, no one has been able to teach a human language to a non-human animal.

It is not just the size of man's brain that allows him to learn language; it is the organization of his brain. Animals with small brains *can* learn language if they are human. Eric Lenneberg has demonstrated this from the case of bird-headed dwarfs. These dwarfs have the same body proportions as normal adults, but they attain a mature height of only two or three feet. As adults, their head circumference and brain weight are those of a normal new-born infant. Yet they are able to master language at least as well as the normal 5-year-old.[37]

Developmental studies of language learning are extremely important in showing the dependence of language learning on biological processes. The language development of every child is remarkably similar regardless of the language, culture, or particular home situation. Some children learn language sooner and faster than others, but the *order* of development is more or less the same for all children, even for retarded children, and is related to other parts of the maturation process. In addition, there are some rather striking differences between the abilities of adults and children to learn languages.[38]

Children begin learning language by naming. These first names are often very generalized categories. Lenneberg gives the examples that "car" might be used for all vehicles, "dog" for all animals, and "daddy" for all people. The child finds some phrase asking "What's that?," and delights in manipulating its environment to find out various names. This first stage of language is limited to approximately fifty words or phrases of three syllables or less, and these elements are never combined. In English, the most common words of the language are the articles "a," "an," and "the" (they account for about 5–10 percent of the words on a given page). But these words never appear among the first words of the child. Syntax is built up in later stages, following pretty much the same developmental pattern in all children. Color naming is a late phenomenon, as is the use of conditional and subjunctive verb phrases.

Children play around with their language, exercising it in both a poetic and metalingual fashion. They try to see what they can do with their language, even when no one is present to reinforce them in any manner. They do this when playing by themselves and when lying in bed before going to sleep.[39]

The development of language continues throughout one's life, of course. College freshmen are capable of a great deal of grammatical refinement, as their professors will affirm. The vocabulary development of high school and college students is nothing short of phenomenal. Slang, added to all the technical and scientific vocabulary amounts to several thousand words each year. A typical 30-year-old Ph.D. probably knows half of the 450,000 words in an unabridged dictionary, and vocabulary development continues in a natural, almost unnoticed fashion as long as one lives and is interested in new things.

Is language learning something magic? Is it automatic upon mere exposure to speech? If I move to a foreign country, will the foreign language automatically grasp hold of my psyche and make me bilingual without any effort on my part? No, language learning is definitely not automatic, not even for children. Americans in foreign countries—both children and adults —frequently fail to learn the local language. In Montreal, children are continually exposed to two languages, but they usually learn only one. Montreal is said to be a city of two unilingualisms rather than a bilingual city. There are severe limitations to the kind of social situation that will result in language learning, and the same is true for the classroom situation. Mere exposure to a foreign language either in the town or in the classroom is no guarantee that a person will learn the language.

Suppose you pipe radio Peking into your child's nursery 24 hours a day. Will he learn Chinese? No. Spoken language, like writing, requires a Rosetta stone. It is the *meaning* of words and sentences that is crucial to language learning. *Languages cannot be learned without a situation of meaningful use.* We can learn foreign languages wherever we can find people to talk with us in those languages, to answer for us the child's questions "What's this?" "Why?" "What does that mean?" But being in the presence of a language is of little help unless we are as active as the child in learning a language, and unless we ask the same kinds of questions.

There is an old myth which says that adults can never be as good at learning languages as children are. Adults have to work at language learning, and, it is said, children do not. Adults inevitably have foreign accents, but children do not. Wilder Penfield suggested that this myth was true, and that it was due to the changes in the brain that occur at adolescence.[40] But the maturation of the brain is not to the adult's disadvantage! The adult can reason more effectively than the child, and this fact actually allows him to learn foreign languages faster than children can. The child might possibly be superior in learning to pronounce, but both in vocabulary and grammar (the ability to say things), the adult is a superior learner. The problem is not that the adult is unable to get to the 5-year-old language level as fast as the 5-year-old can. The adult wants to get to an adult level in the foreign language as fast as the 5-year-old gets to his own level. If educated adults have a vocabulary level of more than 100,000 words in their native language, it is asking a lot to want to become totally bilingual even in 1,000 hours of instruction.

Even in pronunciation, children are over-rated as language learners. Language programs in the elementary schools have found out that children often develop the foreign accent associated with their native tongue and still have to be taught to pronounce correctly, even when they have native speaker teachers to mimic. This is not surprising when we recall that children do not pronounce their own native languages very well at first; it takes quite a while for some children to shake off their "baby talk." Many immigrant children do not lose their foreign accents until after they have experienced the cruel ridicule of their peers. It is true that children are more capable of losing their accents than adults are, but the contrast is made greater because adults are frequently less willing to suppress their foreign accent. Peter Ustinov says that he has no accent when acting in a French movie, but that he cannot speak French without an accent in a face to face conversation. This is a natural phenomenon, because people realize that a foreign accent is their best passport, as Einar Haugen has said.[41] Haugen relates the story of a girl from San Francisco who married a Frenchman. Her pronunciation was so perfect that her acquaintances in France thought she was a rather stupid and uncultured Frenchwoman instead of an exotic foreigner with an exceptionally good knowledge of French. Most adults prefer to retain their foreign identity and their accent.

Except in bilingual localities, we cannot be confident that the earlier we start teaching a foreign language the better. In Cleveland they began teaching foreign languages in the elementary schools to high I.Q. children in 1922. But after several years of experimentation they seemed to be of the opinion that the 7th grade was the optimum time to begin teaching a foreign language, largely because 7th graders could use their powers of reasoning so much more effectively than grade school children could.[42] In three semesters, junior high students can surpass the child with six years study in grade school. But high school students can get to the same point in two semesters, and college students in one semester. Maturity clearly helps one in learning languages faster.

We have been discussing the point that "man is uniquely built to learn languages." The upshot of this discussion is that man actually *learns* languages. Language habits are not just impressed upon us from the outside. But language learning is a very natural and almost effortless activity for the person endowed with curiosity; indeed, it is an activity which we carry on until our death. If foreign language teachers can cooperate with this natural process, we can expect to have both a more enjoyable and a more effective classroom experience.

A Living Language Is a Language in Which We Can Think

We cannot say that we "know" a language until we are able to think in it. Words allow us to represent our non-verbal concepts to ourselves, and to deal abstractly with our experiences. The principles of grammar allow us to "multiply our experience a thousand times" and a thousand times again, and again.

We cannot say that we are bilingual until we can think in two different languages. As a junior in college I spent a great deal of time translating one of Plato's dialogues in my Greek class. When I had finished, I thought that maybe I would be able to read it directly in Greek now that I had translated it. But I couldn't. I was unable to get the meaning of a single sentence without first translating it into English. It would be absurd to say that I was bilingual in Greek and English. Take the example of a singer who sings a concert in faultless German without understanding a word. Or the Latin American politician who reads a speech in perfect English only to resort to using an interpreter in the question and answer period. Again, we cannot say that they are bilingual. Being able to mimic or even to "communicate" does not mean in these cases that the person knows the language that he is using.

After François Gouin failed to learn German, even though he had memorized its grammar, roots, dictionary, and a book of basic German sentences and dialogues, he went back to France and discovered to his chagrin that his 3-year-old nephew had come a long way toward learning French in less than a year. Gouin spent the summer observing his nephew, trying to find the secret of language learning. One day they took a trip to a mill. Gouin describes how the child "went over the mill from top to bottom, he wanted to see everything, to hear the name of everything, to understand about everything. Everything had to be explained to him. . . . He curiously examined the bolters, the millstones, the hoppers. He made the men open the flour store; he pulled back the curtain of the bran room, admired the turning of the pans and belts, gazed with a sort of dread at the rotation of the shafting and the gearing of the cogwheels. . . ."[43]

For an hour after his return home, the child was silent, digesting this experience in his mind. Then he began step by step telling everybody what had happened. Each time he told the story it was slightly different—he would forget details and go back to put them in. But each time he would pass, as Gouin puts it, "from fact to fact, from phrase to phrase, by the same familiar transition, 'and then . . . and then . . .' " The child insisted that Gouin make a water wheel on the small stream near by, and he insisted that his mother make him some small flour sacks. Then he went to his little mill and re-enacted his whole story, filling the bags with sand and telling everyone what he was doing—even repeating it aloud to himself if no one was listening.

This is how a living language is learned—at least at one phase of its development. This is how our experiences are transformed into language. Gouin's nephew learned a large number of words that day—more than he could have learned by rote. Vocabulary in one's native language is not memorized; it is merely learned naturally in a context of real use.

Assume that a 25-year-old speaker of English has a vocabulary of 100,000 words. This means that he has learned an average of more than ten words every day that he has been alive. It is actually a low estimate; he may know more than twice that many words. One might say that this feat of learning is aided by the tremendous redundancy of a language. Once we know *milk* and *man*, we have no trouble learning *milkman*. But we have to learn these compound words nevertheless, or else we would be predicting that a *ginger-*

breadman was the man who delivers gingerbread, and that a *milkmaid* was a feminine milkman. And the redundancy of language does not make it child's play to memorize an arbitrary list of ten Greek words every day. The reason that we can remember vocabulary so easily in a living language is that each new word expresses for us a thought, or it labels a concept which we want to remember. If the word is essential for the thought, we will remember the word. "Association is the fundamental law of memory," says de Sauzé, "we must introduce [the student] very early to a text that expresses thought and not to a haphazard collection of sentences that jump from the cow to the moon and create in the mind of the student the distinct impression that the new language is not capable of conveying thought, but only serves to illustrate grammatical relationship."[44]

No American had trouble learning *defoliation* during the 1964 presidential campaign. *Overkill* and *pre-emptive war* are bothersome concepts, but easy words. The whole world has learned the terminology of spacecraft and rocketry since 1957. Vocabulary learning is an integral part of learning about new things and expressing new thoughts. But memorizing a dictionary does not work. The words are dead, and do not stand for any living concept or thought. Memorizing basic sentences or dialogues is not much better—the language remains basically dead, the words are not our words, the thoughts not our thoughts.

In learning grammar, the same law of association holds in making the rules of grammar psychologically real and alive instead of letting them remain dead abstractions. Memorizing a grammatical rule ("invert subject and verb to make a question") will not give us a correct association for the grammatical processes involved. Neither will a pattern drill. Take the following question formation drill:

TEACHER: John is going home.
STUDENT: Is John going home?

TEACHER: I am reading a book.
STUDENT: Am I reading a book?

The student who is thinking will make a mistake on that drill. He will say to the teacher "Are *you* reading a book?"

Pattern drills require the student to think only about the mechanics of manipulating grammatical structures. He is not required to think in the language when he does a pattern drill. The meaning of the sentence is not very important, and the changes in meaning brought about by the drill make little impression on the student's mind. The foreword to an intermediate book in English as a foreign language acknowledged that "The most difficult transition in learning a language is going from mechanical skill in reproducing patterns acquired by repetition to the construction of novel but appropriate sentences in natural social contexts."[45] Perhaps we can do without this transition by avoiding the first stage altogether. If pattern drills do not instill a living conception of grammar, we should replace them with activities that do. *Language learners need meaningful practice rather than drill.*

The important thing about grammar is that changes in grammatical structure bring about changes in meaning. Unless we can link the structure to the meaning, there is no use in being able to produce the structure. To learn how to form the past tense of the verb, we talk about what we *did* yesterday. To learn the present perfect tense, we talk about what we *have done* in the last several weeks. With this kind of practice, grammar becomes a means of expressing our thoughts, and it becomes a living conception for us.[46]

TEACHING A LIVING LANGUAGE

A living language, by the very definition we have given it, implies the rationalist approach to language learning. For the rationalist, man is a thinking animal and the main function of language is to express our thoughts and to extend our powers of thinking. Behaviorists, on the other hand, do not really believe in 'thinking.' For them, language is behavior, and the main object of this behavior is communication. Some behaviorists even refuse to talk about 'meaning,' because it is so hard to talk about meaning in behavioral terms. To accept the definition of a living language as a language in which we can think, we have to reject the empiricist-behaviorist presuppositions about language learning.

The next chapter will discuss how we can construct a method of foreign language teaching that will teach the student to think in the language from the very beginning. But the underlying principles are these: Language is characterized by rule-governed creativity. If we know the rules of grammar we can create infinitely many new sentences, and we can understand the new sentences which other people say to us. But knowing the language means that the rules are psychologically real to us. We have to know the rules in a functional way, in a way which relates changes in abstract grammatical structure to changes in meaning. Memorizing the formulations of these rules will not result in our having a psychologically real conception of the rules. Memorizing word lists will not make the words be more than dead abstractions for us. Memorizing basic sentences and performing the rote activity of pattern drills is not much better—still the language is treated as a dead language. Man is equipped with a thinking brain that is specially suited to learning *living* languages. Only when we begin practicing how to express real thoughts in a foreign language do we begin treating it as a living language; only then can we begin learning it.

Notes

1. This chapter is based on material in my doctoral thesis (1967), forthcoming in book form as *Linguistic Theories and Language Teaching*.
2. François Gouin, *L'Art d'enseigner et d'étudier les langues*, Paris, Fischbacher, 1880; translated by Howard Swan and Victor Bétis as *The Art of Teaching and Studying Languages*, London, George Philip and Son, 1892, p. 11.
3. *Ibid.*, pp. 26–27.
4. *Ibid.*, pp. 30–31.
5. *Ibid.*, p. 16.
6. John B. Carroll, *The Foreign Language Attainments of Language Majors in the Senior Year*, Cambridge, Harvard University Press, pp. 14, 89.
7. I am using the terms "empiricist" and "rationalist" in the sense defined by Noam Chomsky in *Aspects of the Theory of Syntax*, Cambridge, M.I.T. Press, 1965, pp. 47–48. See also Chomsky's, *Cartesian Linguistics*, New York, Harper & Row, 1966. The term "empiricist" in no way implies a more practical or less dogmatic theory of language acquisition.
8. Leonard Bloomfield, *An Introduction to the Study of Language*, New York, Henry Holt, 1914, p. 14.
9. Harold E. Palmer, *One Hundred Substitution Tables*, Cambridge, W. Heffer and Sons, 1916; *The Scientific Study and Teaching of Languages*, New York, World Book Co., 1917.
10. Einar Haugen, "Linguists and the Wartime Program of Language Teaching," *Modern Language Journal*, Vol. XXXIX, 1955, pp. 243–245. Haugen shows the dependence of American linguist-language teachers on their European predecessors.
11. William E. Rutherford, *Modern English*, New York, Harcourt, Brace, & World, 1968, p. 43.
12. Fe R. Dacanay, *Techniques and Procedures in Second Language Teaching*, Quezon City, Phoenix Publishing House, 1963, p. 144.
13. William G. Moulton, "Linguistics and Language Teaching in the United States 1940–1960," *Trends in European and American Linguistics 1930–1960*, Christine Mohrmann *et al.*, eds., Utrecht, Spectrum, 1961.

14. Eric H. Lenneberg, *Biological Foundations of Language*, New York, John Wiley & Sons, Inc., 1967, pp. 305–309.
15. W. Freeman Twaddell, *On Defining the Phoneme*, Language Monograph No. 16., 1935, reprinted in Joos (See note 22 below), 57n.
16. Leonard Bloomfield, *Language*, New York, Holt, Rinehart, & Winston, 1933, pp. 19–31.
17. Charles F. Hockett, *A Course in Modern Linguistics*, New York, Macmillan, 1958, p. 425.
18. W. Freeman Twaddell, "Meanings, Habits, and Rules," *Education* 49, 1948, pp. 77–78.
19. Moulton, *op. cit.*, p. 89.
20. Archibald A. Hill, "Grammaticality," *Word* 17, 1961, p. 8n.
21. Leonard Bloomfield, *Outline Guide for the Practical Study of Foreign Languages*, Baltimore, Linguistic Society of America, 1942, p. 1.
22. Martin Joos, *Readings in Lingustics: the development of descriptive linguistics in America since 1925*, New York, American Council of Learned Societies, 1958, p. 96.
23. Emile B. de Sauzé, *The Cleveland Plan for the Teaching of Modern Languages*, Philadelphia, John C. Winston, Co., 1929, p. 4.
24. Noam Chomsky, "Linguistic Theory," *Reports of the Working Committees, Northeast Conference on the Teaching of Foreign Languages*, New York, MLA Materials Center, 1966, p. 46.
25. George A. Miller, "The Psycholinguists," *Encounter* 23:1, pp. 29–37, reprinted in *Psycholinguistics*, Charles E. Osgood and Thomas A. Sebeok, eds., Bloomington, Indiana University Press, 1965, p. 299. This estimate does not include the infinite set of sentences containing numbers ("It is at least one second since I began talking," "It is at least two seconds since I began talking" . . .).
26. de Sauzé, *op. cit.*, rev. ed. 1953, p. 5.
27. Bloomfield, *Outline Guide for the Practical Study of Foreign Languages*, p. 13.
28. On distinctive features, see Morris Halle, "Phonology in Generative Grammar," *Word* 18, pp. 54–72, (reprinted in Fodor and Katz, *The Structure of Language*, Englewood

Cliffs, Prentice Hall, 1964); also, Halle, "On the Bases of Phonology," in Fodor and Katz.

29. Jean Berko, "The Child's Learning of English Morphology," *Word* 14, 1958, pp. 150–177. On the Psychological reality of abstract phonological elements, see also Halle, note 28 above, and Edward Sapir, "The Psychological Reality of Phonemes," *The Selected Writings of Edward Sapir*, D. Mandelbaum, ed. Berkeley, University of California Press, 1949; also, Wayne A. O'Neil, "The Reality of Grammars: Some Literary Evidence," paper presented to the Linguistic Circle of New York, 1966.

30. Max Black, *Models and Metaphors: Studies in Language and Philosophy*, Ithaca, Cornell University Press, 1962, p. 101.

31. Patricia O'Connor and W. F. Twaddell, "Intensive Training for an Oral Approach in Language Teaching," *Modern Language Journal*, Vol. XL, No. 2, February, 1960, p. 4.

32. Israel Scheffler, *Conditions of Knowledge*, Chicago, Scott, Foresman, and Co., 1965, p. 105.

33. de Sauzé, *op. cit.*, rev. ed. 1953, p. 14.

34. See note 22.

35. See note 28.

36. See Lenneberg, note 14 for this case and other data pertinent to this paragraph.

37. Lenneberg, *op. cit.*, pp. 69–70.

38. *Ibid.*

39. See Otto Jespersen, *Language, its Nature, Development and Origin*, London, Allen and Unwin, 1922, p. 131; also Ruth Weir, *Language in the Crib*, The Hague, Mouton, 1961.

40. Wilder Penfield, "A Consideration of the Neuro-Physiological Mechanism of Speech and Some Educational Consequences," *Proceedings of the American Academy of Arts and Sciences,* 82, 1953, pp. 201–214.

41. See Einar Haugen, "Bilingualism as a Goal in Foreign Language Teaching," *On Teaching English to Speakers of Other Languages, Series One: Papers read at the TESOL conference, Tucson, Arizona, May, 1964,* Champaign: National Council of Teachers of English.

42. de Sauzé, *op. cit.*, rev. ed. 1953, p. 70.

43. Gouin, *op. cit.*, p. 36.

44. de Sauzé, *op. cit.*, rev. ed. 1953, pp. 9–10.
45. Rutherford, *op. cit.*, foreword by J. Donald Bowen and Robert P. Stockwell, p. vii.
46. The view of grammar learning presented here affirms that the technical apparatus of formal grammatical descriptions is irrelevant. (It might be noted that when Chomsky spoke to language teachers on Linguistic Theory—see note 24 above—he did not even mention such apparatus as phrase structure rules and transformations.) Almost all grammatical descriptions, even the best generative transformational grammars, fail to deal adequately with meaning. The language student is led to understand the rule of grammar from examples, and to formulate the rules primarily in terms of the changes in meaning.

2

Yvone Lenard

METHODS AND MATERIALS, TECHNIQUES AND THE TEACHER

MORE than a decade has elapsed since I began elaborating what was to be named the "verbal-active' method. Dissatisfied with the procedures and results of audio-lingual methods, I hardly wished to regress to the equally inadequate eclecticism of so-called grammar-translation methods with their hodge-podge of concessions to "some" oral training. Instead I decided to attempt a synthesis of teaching methodology that would coherently combine the most promising experiments to date, the hypotheses of the few linguists rejecting the behavioralist-structuralist assumptions, and my many years experience in foreign language teaching. I felt intuitively, moreover, that the new school of thought in linguistics would prove extraordinarily compatible with the best of what had been done in foreign language teaching, as I shall explain. I started by putting everything into question, and then did what we have invited every foreign language teacher to do: consider how a philosophy of language is related to a method of teaching a language and how the principles of a method, conceptual by their very nature, must in turn be given a concrete existence in materials devised to implement a method. I realized that in the teaching of language, the most fundamental question is: "What is language?" There are many possible answers to this

33

question. Acceptance of one answer rather than another determines adherence to one method rather than another, for it is an inescapable fact that a language teaching method is based upon a definition of language, whether that definition be expressed or implied.[1]

Thus, the time-honored and traditional grammar-translation method can be justified only if the answer to "What is language?" is "Language is a collection of graphic symbols"—symbols which must be deciphered (and translated) into the learner's own tongue for transmission over time and distance, a kind of silent, one-way communication of thought. Although this is a true definition, it becomes increasingly apparent that it is unsatisfactory and incomplete. Language exists indeed as written symbol, but long before it becomes a written and read symbol, it is a spoken and heard sound symbol.

Teaching based upon the old method, however good and valid it may be in its own terms, has clearly proved inadequate. This has become so apparent, in fact, that even science is now involved in the teaching of language. And why not? Grammarians and men of letters obviously did not produce competent linguists. When need arose during World War II, it was not the college graduate with a language major, but the boy of French, Italian, or German descent, unlettered if not illiterate, who could converse adequately with native speakers. On the other hand, the college graduate only too often could not carry on a simple conversation in the language he had studied. It seemed that the learning of how to read and write a language, far from representing knowledge of that language, was instead a barrier to the true learning process. Sociologists, anthropologists, and structural linguists were studying and learning the "primitive" languages without the help of grammar, dictionary, or teacher. Their answer to the question, "What is language?" would in effect be "Language is behavior." This means that a given situation will elicit a behavioral response, composed of a certain stream of sound, often accompanied by gestures and facial expressions. Words were lost as separate entities, for they functioned only in relationship to one another. For example, to illustrate: in French, *il n'y a pas de...* may be seen by the grammarian primarily as the negation of *il y a...* , while for the anthropologically oriented observer the morpheme *yapad* uttered in certain situations like *yapad pain, yapad nouvelles,* or *yapad raison* is significant. *Yapad* is considered a pattern of speech to be understood only as an utterance expressing lack, just as "ouch" expresses pain, and has to be memorized as such.

New teaching methods based upon these observations were soon developed; dialogue-pattern methods replaced the old grammar-translation approach. Parrot-like repetition of prefabricated phrases broke the old classroom silence; pattern drills replaced painstaking translation; recitation of verb forms gave way before equally dull substitution drills. A flow of sound filled classroom and language laboratory. But what was being said? Very little, actually. Through these endless hours of repetition, students memorized what Germaine Brée has dubbed "inept, artificially fabricated chit-chat." A disastrous confusion between speaking and reciting was created. *La plume de ma tante est sur le bureau de mon oncle* yielded to *Keskya pour dîner? Des côtelettes et des nouilles*—one utterance as devoid of meaning as the other. Structural linguistics had replaced grammar. All well and good—but it is curious to note that actual classroom communication between teacher and student still took place in English. The contrived pattern dialogues only served in contrived pattern situations.

Is language, then, no more than the utterance of sound? Is the difference between the grunt of the ape and *Keskya pour dîner?* only a relative increase in articulation? Moreover, should we, as teachers of language, be called upon to train a generation of illiterate speakers? And will they ever become speakers? Is this really education, and the only alternative to the grammar-translation method of instruction? Grammar is clearly insufficient for the teaching of language, but can it be replaced by the methods of applied structural linguistics? Many teachers have wondered whether we are not simply proceeding from one error to another.

Years ago, in his Cleveland Plan, Professor Emile B. de Sauzé gave another answer to "What is language?" He based his method on the belief that "Language is invention." It has no existence apart from the speaker or the writer who recreates, reinvents the language for his own needs each time he uses it. It cannot be memorized ready-made; there is no such thing as ready-made language. Learning a language is the discovery of reality in terms of that language. Language is not *part* of culture—*it is* culture. It is what *you* say, and thus it is highly individual; *not* what Frenchmen, or Germans, or Italians may say in a given situation. Unfortunately for the student who has been taught via the pattern drill, the given situation seldom arises. We all know that no two people utter the same words, except perhaps in the most hackneyed expressions of greeting, thanks, or apology. What is worth saying is worth thinking: *Science sans conscience n'est que ruine de l'âme.*

ACQUISITION OF AUTOMATISMS

In spite of these criticisms, it is true that structural linguistics made a very important discovery: the necessity for acquiring automatisms. I am convinced, however, that textbook authors who consider that the acquisition of automatisms will be made through memorization of dialogues are incorrectly applying a sound idea. The only automatism to be acquired in this way is that of the verb in its question-answer form. It is the only part of speech in which the automatism will be of general use. The sentence arranges itself around the verb. In the complex sentence of the dialogues the important point is lost. Let students acquire those automatic question-answer forms of the verbs, for example, in French, starting with the most common and the most difficult, *être* and *avoir*.

Linguists will counter with the argument that people do not speak with these pat forms. To the question: *"Avez-vous faim?"* they will not necessarily answer: *"Oui, j'ai faim."* They may say any number of things, like *"Oui"* or *"Et comment!"* or *"Je meurs de faim!"* or even stray as far as *"Qu'est-ce qu'on la saute!"* Precisely. The only answer, then, must be: *"Oui, j'ai faim,"* since the others vary so widely. Let's put first things first. How could we ask our students to memorize such highly subjective answers, and of such limited value? We should teach the "automatic," valid one and proceed from there.

The Verb in Its Question-Answer Form

The fixed element of language, the only one worth memorizing or acquiring as a reflex, is thus the correspondence between the question form of the verb and its answer form. At the elementary level of language, the constant in any question-answer group of sentences is the verb. To illustrate, in French, *Avez-vous?* will elicit *J'ai* or *Je n'ai pas*, whatever the rest of the sentence may be. And the answer to *Aviez-vous?* will be *J'avais* or *Je n'avais pas*, and nothing else. This is true for almost all verbs. *Faire* is the most notable exception, but even then, if the verb used in the answer is different, the tense remains the same as in the question: *Qu'est-ce que vous ferez? J'irai en vacances.*

It is, therefore, imperative that the student learn to listen for the verb in the sentence, recognize its form, and answer immediately with the appropriate form. In my textbooks and laboratory materials, I heavily emphasize *...-vous? -Je...* rather than put equal emphasis on all persons. For one thing, this combination is the most difficult, the only one to require a consistent change of form; other persons require only a different order: *Etes-vous? je suis*, but *Sommes-nous? nous sommes* or *Est-il? il est* or *Sont-ils? ils sont.*

It is also extremely important to spend a good deal of time and practice on the verbs "to be" and "to have" before others are introduced; they are the most commonly used and also the most difficult, particularly for the ear. In French, *il a, elle a; il est, elle est;* and *ils sont, ils ont* are hard to distinguish at first by the novice. Learning to understand these two verbs and to use them without hesitation will lay a solid working foundation. Not only are they essential to all simple sentences, as well as more complex ones, but they are used in a myriad of expressions, of which *avoir faim, soif, peur, envie, tort, raison, besoin* are only a few examples. They are also, of course, the key to the seemingly complicated system of compound tenses: *Avez-vous? J'ai* or *Je n'ai pas* will lead to *Avez-vous fini? Oui, j'ai,* or *Non, je n'ai pas fini.* Further, *Aviez-vous? Oui, j'avais* or *Non, je n'avais pas* will lead to *Aviez-vous fini? Oui, j'avais* or *Non, je n'avais pas fini.* Note that when considered in this way, the problem of word order and place of negation does not even exist.

The learning of verbs is done primarily through the question-answer form, always in a sentence, never alone. When all forms have been learned and used, and habits acquired, arrangement of the forms in the standard order of the conjugation paradigm may or may not be given. It is, in any case, little more than a summing up.

A few other patterns of speech are important and useful and should be learned as such; they should not, however, involve complete sentences to be memorized but should be morphemic groups like *il y en a* or *il n'y en a pas*, since they are to be used immediately and repeatedly by the student in his own sentences.

FROM THEORY TO PRACTICE

Great ideas can be re-examined in a different light; re-explored in another context they remain valid. This is their hallmark. Where they were once conclusions, they may become points of departure. So it is that our method owes a heavy debt to de Sauzé, whose ideas about teaching language as both a skill and a humanity were put in practice in the Cleveland Plan. As a point of departure I have taken de Sauzé's principles of multiple approach and single emphasis, and I have sought their fullest application, although after working with these ideas and experimenting with various techniques, I often reach conclusions different from his. The manner in which I propose to apply them is often at great variance with de Sauzé's.

Single Emphasis

Single emphasis consists of teaching one thing at a time, and one thing only—with the constant incorporation of what was previously learned. This is, of course, also the basic idea of programmed instruction. Complexities in the material can always be broken down into component parts, each of which is simple enough for easy mastery. A familiar structure always serves to introduce a new one, always in conjunction with previously learned vocabulary. Vocabulary, in turn, serves to enlarge the means of expression thus acquired. Single emphasis requires a highly controlled and disciplined system, while constantly drawing upon the powers of imagination and invention. Students soon learn that *Une bonne composition est correcte, originale, intéressante, probablement élégante. Et, surtout, pas de dictionnaire.*

A careful application of the rule of single emphasis is essential if the speaking skill is to develop as rapidly as possible, for although the student can certainly understand intellectually even the most complex elements of structure, his performing skill does not match his passive comprehension. Many instructors have deplored the fact that their third-semester students "knew so much about, and could do so little with" the language. Awareness of this fact is essential at all levels, but particularly during the first few lessons. The performance expected from the student, that is, his answering and speaking, must not include more than one new element at a time. To illustrate, although a student may understand the difference between *de, des, du,* and correctly do fill-in exercises with the help of his book, he cannot master their use in speech all at once. Through single emphasis, he will learn how to use *de: C'est la voiture de M. Martin;* in another lesson, he will learn *du: C'est la voiture du jeune homme;* later, he will learn *des,* as the plural of *un: J'ai des frères.* Still later, he will use *des* as the contraction of *de + les.*

Multiple Approach

The multiple approach reunites the four superficially distinct bands of language: audio, lingual, visual, and graphic. Each is used to reinforce the others. The components of language cannot be divorced from one another. They are, in the strictest sense, interdependent.

It seems obvious that language must first be understood, then spoken; habits and mechanisms of speech are essential, too. Learning how to read and write, far from being a hindrance to speech, will act instead as strong reinforcement *if* it is done concurrently with—not before, or weeks or months later—learning how to speak. The student already knows how to read and write his own language, and try as he may, he cannot disregard that fact in learning the foreign language. To wit, the pathetic attempts audio-lingual students constantly make to transcribe what they are required to memorize into "free form" phonetics of their own. There is enough logic even in the spelling of French, unphonetic as it may sometimes be, so that a great deal of the writing can be deduced from sounds, rather than taught from the sight of words. And even though at first only so-called "simple" language is involved, it is certainly not true that simple language is synonymous with simple minds and childish thoughts. A ready example of this is Descartes' classic *"Je pense, donc je suis."*

Learning How to Write

In the course of our experience, we have found that the generally accepted order of hear-speak/read-write should be modified to hear-speak/write-read, with writing preceding any reading. This is precisely one of the features of our method that achieves spectacular results: teaching students how to write from sound. Again, French has, obviously, its own logic for transcribing sounds into symbols. Starting this way, from inside the language, rather than from the outside, you can train your students to use this logic.

The Vowels

It is actually the sound of the vowels that supplies the most important clue to the writing of French. Say to your students *"A est une voyelle. Répétez A."* Have the class repeat several times after you. Then, name the five vowels *A E I O U* slowly several times, with the class repeating them after you. Do not write them. Send a student to the board, and ask him to write *A E I O U.* He may hesitate a little, but he will eventually write them, encouraged by others. Ask another to write *E I A I E O U I A E E A I U E A O.* As soon as he does not hesitate anymore, let him return to his seat. Ask the class to read aloud the letters on the board. Send another, and another, until a fair sampling of the class shows that the vowels have been mastered.

Naturally, phonetically speaking, there are sixteen, not five, vowels in French, but we are not trying to orient the student toward phonological linquistics. We are training him to use a familiar concept of written language, which he will find infinitely more helpful in the beginning than if he were to learn the phonetic symbols of all sixteen vowels. The generative principle can be applied to learning how to write from an understanding of the inner logic of the graphic system of the given language. The five alphabetical vowels (plus "*y*") are the elements which represent orthographically all the vowel sounds, and learning "*eu*" is not a more difficult symbolical process than learning [ø] or [œ] for the language novice. The use of the phonetic alphabet may eventually be helpful, but its incorporation of small Roman characters can lead to confusions as numerous as the distinctions it makes possible.

The Alphabet

Say "*L'alphabet français*," and recite the alphabet slowly, pausing after each letter so that the class can repeat it. Then, proceed in the same manner as for the vowels. Send a student to the board to write the alphabet under your dictation. Send others to write letters at random. Of course, you will emphasize those which are difficult, like *J* and *G, Y, H,* and the vowels already learned. Send several students in quick succession to write vowels and consonants until you are sure everyone can write them from dictation or read them aloud.

An amusing exercise at this point is to have some students dictate their initials, for example, to another who writes them on the board. Make them understand what you want by writing your own name, underlining each initial and saying "*C'est l'initial.*" This has an advantage: the one who dictates will tolerate no error on the part of the writer, since it involves personal, and therefore important, information. Let the students struggle to achieve meaningful communication in this way. After a few minutes, the correspondence between sound and symbol will be firmly established.

The Syllable

Since French words can be divided into syllables and since most syllables are open, that is, end with a vowel, it is extremely important that students learn how to write the individual syllables as a step toward writing the word.

Send a student to the board, and ask him to write *l* and *e*, then *le*, *l* and *a*, then *la*. Do the same thing for *lo, lu, li*. Another will write *de, du, di, da;* another *me, mi, ne, te, se, si, so, ta, tu*, etc. You can see the immense importance of this simple exercise. Always have other students read aloud what has been written on the board.

The Word

Now, dictate a few simple words to students at the board: *la cape, la rose, le tigre, l'animal, l'ami, la robe, etc.* Limit yourself to easy words, with phonetic spelling. From then on, each day, send students to the board to write what they have said or heard. Have them repeat the latter aloud before writing it. Writing must never be allowed to replace speaking. Teach the letter-group sounds one at a time in the following manner:

One day, teach the letter-group sound *-eau* (also spelled *-au*). Write it, circle it, send a student to write, for example, *C'est un beau chapeau*, and another to write *C'est le tableau de la classe*. Do not teach it in a vacuum, but always when the need arises, because the words to be learned that day include this letter-group. For *-oi* you might use *C'est moi, voilà le roi, le toit* (you say: *"avec t final"*) *du garage*.

Do not hesitate, as you encounter more difficult words, to spell out anything that does not conform to phonetic spelling; but whenever possible, guide the students by referring them to something that they already know for comparison: *demain* is *de* and *main; belle* is like *elle* after a *b*. You will no doubt enjoy this test of your own ingenuity.

Of course, there are problems in French spelling that cannot be avoided with this system, although many will be. You will have to give certain spellings as a matter of fact—*temps, doigt,* etc. However, students will easily accept them and will see enough logic to the spelling of French to make its learning an active, intelligent process.

As time passes and as new words appear, you may, of course, occasionally write them yourself on the board. But, whenever possible, have the students write the words themselves, always in the context of a sentence in which the new word is the only new element: Have the students write *mardi, mercredi, samedi;* then show them the spelling of the sound *un,* and ask for *lundi.*

Accent Marks

You will not want to teach the entire diacritical system at one time. Start by writing *e,* have it repeated—it is the mute *e* —and then put an acute accent on it—*é.* Pronounce it, then have it repeated, watching out for the diphthong. Next, ask a student to write *le téléphone, l'étudiante, la clé, la générosité,*

The same day, or the next day if you prefer, proceed in a similar manner with *è.* Emphasize the fact that it occurs on the *e* followed by a consonant and a mute *e: è + consonant + e* at the end of a word—*la mère, le frère, la pièce, je pèse, j'achète,* etc. Not only is this true, but it is an absolute rule. It is true for nouns, adjectives, verbs. If you succeed in making this quite clear to your students, you will have solved many future problems, among them the vexing question of the shifting and changing accents on certain verbs of the first conjugation like *j'espère, je lève, j'achète.*

The circumflex accent can be presented in the same way. Wait to teach it until you encounter a word that needs it: *la fenêtre,* for example. Point out that it sounds like *è* and that it generally occurs before a *t: la forêt, la tête.*

Do not worry about what you did not have time to do today. Think instead of the importance of what your students have learned. They will never confuse *de* and *du;* they have learned the system of accents; they know that the feminine of *premier* and *dernier* are spelled *première* and *dernière,* to cite just a few examples. You have taught them basic, infinitely useful things to carry them through their study of French. And you still have not spoken any English, nor does the class feel the need for any.

I can indicate here only a few of the elements of the teaching of writing. But if your class is in the proper frame of mind, actively thinking and correlating the various aspects of language, you will have no trouble discovering, improvising, and perfecting, and each day you can add a new element to the whole organic structure of sound turned into written symbol.

TEACHING IN THE FOREIGN LANGUAGE

Instruction can and must be carried out in the foreign language, provided the instructor uses it wisely, with clarity and great simplicity from the very first day. This is evidenced by the success obtained by those teachers who faithfully speak only the target language during the foreign language class period. An occasional exception may have to be made in pre-college level classes, as is explained in the last chapter, where the teacher is responsible for administrative duties outside the actual teaching of the foreign language. Explaining in English that we must speak French, for example, is obviously self-defeating, and speaking English during the first term will not make proficient second-term speakers. Time gained by speaking English is actually time lost.

Students, moreover, are anxious to hear and to speak the foreign language. You need say very little at first outside of the actual words of the lesson. Choose your words carefully at first, use cognates, make simple statements. *"Excellent! Correct! Horrible! C'est une classe de français,"* etc., need no translation. Stylize your reactions: enthusiastic approval, serious doubt, horrified surprise. The point is to establish meaningful communication, without English, and with a little of the target language. Avoid using words or structures the students cannot possibly understand. This is always possible, and there is always another, simpler way to say what you mean.

It is very important not to allow students to use English. They may, at first, be a little self-conscious, or insecure, and try to translate just "to make sure." We all know that if they went to live in France, they would learn French if they wanted to, and they would get no translation. Be good-natured and pleasant about it, but very firm. The success of the whole term depends on those first few days.

Although the foreign language is used as the exclusive means of instruction, I want to emphasize that this method is not to be confused with eclectic and unsystematic so-called "direct" methods. It is not direct in the generally understood meaning of "directly in contact with the foreign language," a situation where there are not necessarily any rules of procedure. Ours *is* a very rational direct method, however, a highly systematized programing, going from the simplest unit of language to the most complex through carefully calculated steps. And yet it gives the student a feeling of great freedom, of an endless possibility of expression and experimentation within an orderly framework.

Learning Versus Covering the Material

Learning does not mean covering a certain amount of material. It is not acquiring the ability to recognize a word or form and translate it painstakingly into English. It is acquiring the ability to understand or use freely and spontaneously what has been studied as a means of expression, spoken or written.

The amount of vocabulary, especially in the first lessons, should be limited, and the student is never expected to memorize long lists of words. No doubt more words could be taught, but the vocabulary, in order to be active, must be limited and, at the beginning, strictly controlled. One must concentrate on the acquisition of basic automatisms of structure before allowing the vocabulary to expand. If students are to acquire the speaking skill, there must be overlearning of the basics. It is far better to go more slowly and study fewer lessons than to go too fast and be forced to spend the following term reviewing what was not learned in the first place.

Above all, a method, its techniques, and its materials must be *student-centered,* as opposed to text-centered. The text must not be "reified," turned into a *res,* the "thing" to be learned. Everything must be geared to and promote actual meaningful communication. A foreign language class should be conducted with books closed. Discourage the taking of notes in class, unless there seems to be a special reason, such as when you are introducing vocabulary items which are not in the lesson, or when you are giving examples which do not appear in the book. Absolutely forbid the use of a dictionary in first-year classes. A text should be intended only to show students how the structures they are learning actively will combine and form the expressions and style of the foreign language. Emphasis should be placed on the fact that it is what the student can do with what he has learned from the text that interests us. Studying the book is a means, not an end.

Teaching Vocabulary

Isolated words are, of course, of no interest whatsoever, and vocabulary should always be taught in context. How can one teach new vocabulary without using English? In the first few lessons, you can either show, for example, and in French, *une jeune fille, un tableau, une fenêtre,* etc., or show a picture or draw a quick sketch of *un chien, un chat, une maison, un arbre,* etc., or rely on the resemblance between cognate words—*un professeur, un appartement, une auto, un téléphone, un restaurant,* etc. A little later, you can explain the new word from words students already know; *un im-*

meuble, for instance: *"Un immeuble est un bâtiment avec beaucoup d'appartements."* Sometimes a quick sketch confirms the students' impression of having understood. New words may also be explained by means of cognates *(la réclame, c'est la publicité)*; often they can be explained as *le contraire de quelque chose*, particularly in the case of adjectives *(facile est le contraire de difficile, laid est le contraire de beau, ou de joli)*. When possible, it is better to explain generic terms by example rather than abstract explanation *(le fromage: le Roquefort est un fromage)*. In many cases, your ingenuity will be tested, and in others you will be delighted to hear some of your students' own definitions. You can often call on students who have understood your definition to give their own to those who have not. Give many examples for the use of words you consider important, send students to write those words on the board, etc. Do not waste too much time on cognates—except for frequent *faux amis*, e.g., *actuellement, audience*—for they will be easily learned.

One may ask if this is not quite a waste of time, since it would be so much faster to translate. We would reply most emphatically not. You want your students to discover reality in terms of the target language and the object to take on a new identity in terms of its foreign language expression. (We all know, as one of my students pointed out, that *une algue* does not bring to mind the same picture as "seaweed.") Besides, throughout all this so-called "waste of time," we are communicating and conversing with our students in the target language, using all they have previously learned in order to learn more. Is there any sounder pedagogical exercise?

Introducing a New Structure

Suppose you want to introduce the negation. Your students already know *C'est un . . . c'est une. . . .* Pick up a book, for instance, and ask: *"Qu'est-ce que c'est?"* The class will answer: *"C'est un livre."* Next, pick up an object which they cannot name yet in French, for instance, a key, and ask: "*Qu'est-ce que c'est?*" You will have no answer. So, you wait a second, and, with the dramatic manner which you reserve for the introduction of a new element, a manner which the class has already learned to recognize and to identify with "something new to learn," you say: "*Ce n'est pas un livre.*" Have the class repeat. You ask then, "*Est-ce un livre?*" and the class will answer, "*Non, ce n'est pas un livre.*" Then, going fast, pick up or point to various objects, asking: "*Est-ce une fenêtre? Est-ce une chaise? Est-ce une auto?*" etc., all requiring negative answers. Then, with a slight dramatic pause and your "Now, be careful!" look, start mixing questions which require positive and negative answers: "*Est-ce une jeune fille? Non, ce n'est pas... ; Est-ce un jeune homme? Oui, c'est...* " etc.

Besides the choral responses which you want at the introduction of a new point, make sure that everyone in the class has spoken individually as often as possible. Choral responses mean little as far as individual participation is concerned. Then, send a student to the board to write what he has just said. Have the class watch, check, correct, if necessary, by explaining to him in the target language what his errors are. You, the teacher, will do a minimum of writing on the board. Instead, send the students to write what they have just said or what someone else has just said. But again, remember: never let them replace speaking with writing.

Exercises

Exercises should be prepared at home, written, preferably, and done in class orally. It would be best if the student could do them without referring to his preparation. Or, have the students hand them in first, then do them orally, sending students to the board to write only points which seem to present a difficulty.

The Oral Composition

The oral composition is a very important factor in the success you will obtain with our method. There should be one for every lesson, to be followed the next day by a written one. The oral composition becomes, in fact, the most important exercise of the verbal-active method in building the elements of which fluency is composed: the ability to speak at length, aloud, clearly and confidently, in front of other people, and to use the words and structures that you know freely and correctly in order to say what you mean. It is such an integral part that I shall outline here the procedure in some detail:

After completing each lesson, assign an oral composition for the next day. You should use your imagination, as well as the circumstances of your class, in suggesting topics suited to the particular situation, place, group interest, and age level.

The oral composition should be short at the beginning, perhaps an average of ten lines, and become progressively longer. It should not become much longer than a page, but it ought to become increasingly complex, and the teacher should require more and more in richness and variety of expression.

When you assign the subject: *"Voilà la composition orale pour demain,"* write down the subject or subjects on the board. *Une excellente composition est originale, imaginative, correcte. Dictionnaire? Non, non, absolument non.*

This is the first time that students may be seriously tempted to use the dictionary, so that it is quite important to forbid it now. No need to say that looking up words in a dictionary at this point would be disastrous. If anyone breaks the rule, you will have no difficulty recognizing it; since students have little experience in the language, they will pick out any word from the different choices and come up with some hair-raising French. The boy who wrote *Je suis ventilateur de cinéma* was genuinely surprised that the instructor could tell he had looked up the word "fan." Other examples are given in the last chapter of this book. Deal sternly with offenders; you might even suggest *la guillotine*.

You may give indications and suggestions on what you consider to be a good composition. For example, you may say: "*Composition orale. Ecrivez la préparation, mais dans la classe, vous parlez, et le papier est dans la serviette. La composition est approximativement dix lignes* (pick up a note book and show what you mean), *sur le sujet 'Description de la classe de français.' Voilà un exemple: Dans la classe de français, M. X est derrière moi et Mlle Y est devant moi. Elle est sur une chaise. Le professeur est sur une chaise derrière le bureau, entre la porte et la fenêtre. Il est à côté du tableau. La serviette du professeur est par terre. Le professeur est une dame, mais le mot 'professeur' est masculin. C'est Madame Y, le professeur de français de la classe,*" etc. You will be pleasantly surprised to find that your students' imagination is excellent and that they manage to say quite a bit with the little they know.

The next day, before asking for individual compositions, explain (it will not be difficult) that after the composition you would like some students to ask questions of others on what they have just heard. It may be the boys who will ask questions of the girls, or vice versa, or one side of the room of the other, or names chosen at random—any way you like best, as long as the largest possible number of students participates.

During the individual compositions, register enthusiastic approval of the student who has done exactly what you wished and is "speaking"—you do not allow reading—a simple, varied, imaginative short composition clearly, using as much of what he has learned as possible. Those who have already studied some French may try to use complicated structures, words or forms that the rest of the class has not yet learned. They will probably make mistakes; so speak to them after class and explain why they must try to use only what everyone else is learning. Otherwise, they will make no progress and

La Voyelle et La Consonne

—Voyelle, êtes-vous française?

—Oui, Consonne, je suis française.

—L'accent circonflexe est très joli, mademoiselle. C'est un bon costume. Il est très pratique. Comment vous appelez-vous, mademoiselle?

—Je m'appelle Mademoiselle ê. Je suis dans la fenêtre et dans la tête.

—Tu es une amie, mademoiselle. Nous sommes dans la fenêtre et la tête. Je m'appelle Madame T.

—Quelle heure est-il, Madame T?

—Il est neuf heures, Mademoiselle ê.

—Neuf heures! L'alphabet est avec la classe de français.

—Terrible! Nous sommes absentes.

(handwritten draft of the above composition, titled "Une Composition — La Voyelle et La Consonne")

Mon animal favori

. . . "Georges" n'est pas un nom ordinaire pour un chat, mais Georges n'est pas un chat ordinaire.

Quelquefois, Georges a l'air féroce, mais en réalité, il est gentil. Il n'est pas timide. Georges est très bavard, parce qu'il est un chat siamois. Il a un vocabulaire considérable, pour un chat. Il est très intelligent, et sa compagnie est agréable.

Son lit est la chaise favorite de mon père. Mon père n'est pas l'ami de Georges. "Je voudrais bien avoir ma chaise, Georges, s'il vous plaît," dit-il. Georges a l'air très désagréable. "Miaou," dit à moi, "votre père a mauvais caractère."

(handwritten draft of the above composition, titled "Composition — Mon Animal favori")

Mon animal favori est un rat blanc. Je n'ai pas de rat aujourd'hui. Hélas! Il est mort, mais il est dans ma mémoire.

(handwritten draft titled "Mon animal favori")

These samples demonstrate the progressive stages of facility in written French acquired by students at Stanford University.

Deux amis habitent Balboa et ils disent que c'est elle est une bonne idée parce qu'il y a beaucoup de jeunes filles sur la plage à Balboa. Mes amis et moi, nous comparé! la plage où nous faisons de la natation, des promenades ??? étudions des jeunes filles. (une leçon d'anatomie ???)

Nous allons trouver une petite maison au bord de la mer naturellement. nous allons donner beaucoup de partis merveilleuse. Nos amis vont venir et leurs amis aussi. tous nos amis nouveaux

Deux amis habitent Balboa et ils disent que visiter leur ville est une bonne idée parce qu'il y a beaucoup de belles jeunes filles sur la plage à Balboa. Mes amis et moi aiment la plage où nous faisons de la natation, des promenades ou étudions des jeunes filles. ????

Nous allons trouver une petite maison au bord de la mer et, naturellement, nous allons donner beaucoup de parti merveilleux. Nos amis vont venir et leurs amis aussi, et tous nos amis nouveaux.

Quelquefois, je préfère la musique de Beethoven; quelquefois je préfère la musique de Bach — ou quelquefois je trouve le jazz le plus agréable (mais c'est une occasion rare). En un mot, la musique que je préfère écouter dépend de ma disposition). Par exemple, quand le soir est romantique et je voudrais rester tranquille, je trouve la musique impressionniste merveilleuse

. . . Quelquefois, je préfère la musique de Beethoven; quelquefois je préfère la musique de Bach—ou quelquefois je trouve le jazz le plus agréable (mais c'est une occasion rare). En un mot, la musique qui je préfère écouter dépend de ma disposition. Par exemple, quand le soir est romantique et je voudrais rester tranquille, je trouve la musique impressionniste merveilleuse.

Mais il y a plus de peus choses intéressantes dans l'auditoire que sur l'écran au film de James Bond. Pendant que James Bond poursuit les criminels avec des coups de revolver, toutes les hommes, vieux ou jeunes, ont l'air d'action, leurs pensées dans une autre monde. Les maris tout à coup pensent que leurs femmes ont de la bonne chance d'être marié avec eux.

Mais ce n'est pas tout. Pendant que Monsieur Bond embrasse une de ses jeunes filles, il y a un grand souffle dans l'auditoire — toutes les jeunes filles et les femmes sont, à ce moment-ci, dans les bras de James Bond. La scène est très drôle.

Les films de James Bond

. . . Mais il y a plus choses intéressantes dans l'auditoire que sur l'écran au film de James Bond. Pendant que James Bond poursuit les criminals avec des coups de revolver, tout les hommes, vieux ou jeunes, ont l'air d'action, leurs pensées dans une autre monde. Les maris tout à coup pensent que leurs femmes ont de la bonne chance d'être marié avec eux.

Mais ce n'est pas tout. Pendant que Monsieur Bond embrasse une de ses jeunes filles, il y a un grand souffle dans l'auditoire—toutes les jeunes filles et les femmes sont, à ce moment-ci, dans les bras de James Bond. La scène est très drôle.

These are quotations from oral compositions by beginning
students of French at the University of California, Los Angeles.

On arriving on time:

"Il faut être à l'heure, mais si on est à l'heure, les autres ne sont pas là pour le voir . . ."

"Quand je suis à l'heure, tout le monde est surpris et dit: 'Mon Dieu, Carolyn est sûrement malade . . .' "

"Être ou ne pas être, voilà la chose importante. Mais être à l'heure ou ne pas être à l'heure est une chose relative et sans importance . . ."

What did you do during vacation?:

"J'ai travaillé pendant les vacances. Ce n'était pas un travail difficile, quelquefois il était même amusant. Je vendais des bijoux-fantaisie dans un grand magasin. J'en ai vendu beaucoup, surtout à des jeunes filles qui allaient à des soirées . . ."

"C'était peut-être des vacances pour vous, mais pas pour moi. Je travaillais dans une équipe de construction. Il y avait de mauvais moments, mais aussi d'autres qui étaient formidables . . ."

On using two (or more) verbs together:

"J'ai appris à jouer du piano quand j'avais huit ans. Maintenant, je voudrais bien apprendre à parler français . . ."

"Quand on est sportif, on aime faire tous les sports. Mais je ne suis pas très sportif, je préfère lire, écouter de la musique, sortir avec des amis. J'aime bien aussi regarder les sports à la télévision et donner des conseils aux joueurs . . ."

"Des amis qui ont visité l'Europe sont arrivés hier à l'aérodrome. Alors, je suis allé les y chercher. L'avion était en retard, mais enfin, je les ai vu descendre . . ."

On the use of <u>falloir</u> in its different tenses:

"Il faudrait que j'étudie un peu plus. Mais chaque fois que je m'installe à mon bureau, le téléphone sonne, et il faut bien que j'y réponde . . ."

"Il aurait fallu que le Président puisse deviner ou au moins prévoir l'avenir; mais il ne faudrait pas le blâmer maintenant s'il faut qu'il fasse des actions et prenne des décisions que nous n'approuvons pas . . ."

will keep on repeating those errors which have prevented their progress in the first place.

When what you expect has been made clear to everyone by your approval of those compositions which meet your standards, by discouraging the overambitious one, the overly simple one, the one that does not say anything (e.g., *Voilà une classe. Voilà un étudiant. Voilà un bureau*, etc.), you will obtain good compositions from nearly all the students, although they will be as different from one another as the students themselves. This is one of the great achievements of this method—it cultivates originality, free invention, and personal expression within a strictly controlled structural framework.

After each composition has been delivered, ask for questions based on what has been said. At first these will be simple: *Est-ce que le professeur est une dame? Où est la serviette de Mlle X? Où est M. Z dans la classe de français?* They will, like the compositions, increase in complexity as the course progresses. In this way, you have the whole group participating. Occasionally ask a student to write on the board something that someone has just said. Correct, or ask the class to correct, the sentence. Remember, it is much better that students write on the board than you do. Questions and answers are asked and given; it is an active, not a passive exercise for the whole class.

You may certainly have the student stand in front of the class when giving his oral composition. I prefer to let him stay in his seat so that it does not assume the proportions of a speech. The only trick is that, wherever the student is seated, you walk to the opposite end of the room; if he is seated in the front row, stand at the back of the room. This will force him, in order to face you, to face the whole class; and if you can hear him from where you are, everyone else can too.

Depending on the size of the class, you may or may not be able to hear all the compositions. But you must make sure everyone has spoken, if only to ask or answer questions.

The assignment for the following day is then the written composition.

The Written Composition

There is no point in writing, that is, in permanently recording, anything that has not yet reached its best possible form. This is one of several reasons why written composition follows oral. When all possible improvements have been made in the oral work in class, when students have been corrected by you, learned from one another, and gained new ideas from what they have heard, then, and only then, is it time for them to go home and write. It is not necessary, of course, that the written composition be an exact reproduction of the oral composition.

Be strict at first, until good habits are acquired, not only as far as the content of the composition is concerned, but in its presentation as well. You want the date in French; you want the subject of the composition written out at the top of the page; you want either a wide margin or alternate lines of writing, so as to leave room for corrections. Accents must be used correctly and the writing must be neat. Make these requirements clear by showing to the class the compositions you consider well presented.

In correcting compositions, do not overcorrect. Correct only actual mistakes, and if the sentence needs rebuilding, use only those words or structures which the student knows and can understand. Express great enthusiasm when returning the graded papers, for those which show that students have profited by corrections or additions made during oral compositions. This will help others get the idea. In French schools outstanding work is read aloud to the class, and the student named. I find it a good practice to read at least those parts which I consider excellent, pointing out what causes my enthusiasm. Never exclude the weak student from this distinction. Whenever he has written at least something good, praise him publicly. Always try, difficult as it may be, to return compositions the next day or as soon as possible, while they are fresh in the students' minds. This keeps the excitement of the class alive.

Presenting Textbook Reading Selections

I do not think it is advisable in elementary college language classes to spend class time on reading aloud from the book or on having students read aloud from the book. Reading aloud in a foreign language is a difficult exercise, hard to perform satisfactorily because of the interference of the native graphic and sound systems. Texts are seldom intended to be read aloud. In the course of our experience, we either speak aloud to communicate or read silently to understand.

There are several ways to present a reading selection:

1. Tell the "story" to the class. It does not have to be a word-for-word repetition. In the case of one of my own reading selections—a simple passage involving four young people. I would find, among my students, four who answer the description of the four characters in the reading and build up a story around them. I may not have a French André, but I will surely have *un jeune homme brun sympathique,* who instead of being *français* will be *il n'est pas français.* I keep asking many questions; I send students to the board to write what they have said, especially sentences involving new words.

2. Excellent tape recordings should be available to accompany readings. They must be lively, dramatic, and include interesting sound effects and a variety of voices. It is very effective to play this kind of tape on a simple tape recorder right in the classroom after you have made the story and the new words clear.

In any case, books should be closed, of course, with the exception of yours, at which you may glance occasionally. Here, again, you have an active, general participation involving performance by the student in a strictly oral milieu, with writing from sound used occasionally to fix and reinforce.

After a reading has been presented in this manner, you may assign it as an exercise to do at home and ask that the questions following it be prepared for the next day. You will soon realize that students enjoy rediscovering on the printed page the words and meanings that they have already acquired in the active experience and presentation of the classroom. This early experience is thus a true reading experience, and the student is positively conditioned for more difficult reading later on.

The Language Laboratory

There are many kinds of laboratory equipment, as well as many systems of laboratory administration. You are, of course, the best judge of the possibilities of your system and the best use that can be made of it under the conditions in your school. We will make only some general suggestions for the proper use of the laboratory with our method.

The laboratory should never be used for initial learning, but only for practice, habit building, or overlearning.

Do not allow the students to hear the tape until the lesson has been completed in class.

Although the laboratory can be a useful testing instrument, this is not where its greatest value lies. The laboratory is essentially a learning instrument. It is to oral language what a library is to written language. The great potential of the laboratory lies precisely in the fact that it can make the sound of the foreign language available at all times for as many repetitions as needed. To reap the greatest possible benefits from a laboratory, it should be used as a library, open as long as possible, and students should be encouraged to spend all the time there that they need. If, on the contrary, the class goes to the laboratory as a group, you will find yourself, by the very nature of circumstances, in a situation similar to that of testing, since the time element is controlled. In a learning situation, on the other hand, the result is all that matters, and not the time that it has taken to achieve it. If, for administrative or technical reasons, it is impossible to use the laboratory in this manner, then the next best solution would be to schedule at least two half-hour sessions a week.

In any case, laboratory time must be scheduled in addition to class time and not be deducted from it. The laboratory hour is a time for practice; it is oral homework. Make sure that adequate scheduling of the laboratory, as well as class hours, has been made and that students understand that laboratory time is part of the homework you require for the course.

A laboratory workbook is an immensely helpful tool for both student and instructor. The student should hear the tape at least once and do all the exercises orally. Then, when he has acquired some degree of familiarity with the tape material, play the tape again while he does his laboratory exercises in writing.

Dictation

Dictation is a valuable exercise. If you have a laboratory, why not save class time and have dictation there? If you do not have a laboratory, you may schedule a dictation periodically. Always be sure the dictation uses what you have been teaching rather than oddities or exceptions.

TESTING

Testing should, of course, be both oral and written, and in grading, it seems fair to me to accord equal importance to oral and written achievement.

Written Tests

If you are using the verbal-active method, you are keeping your hand on the pulse of the class, so to speak. You hear everyone speak frequently, and you see and hear numerous compositions; in short, testing will have a different value than, say, in a lecture class.

You will probably want to give a written test once a month, or every four or five lessons. The test should be composed entirely in the target language. The mid-term will probably be your second test of the semester. You should give another test a few lessons later and the final examination at the end of the semester. If you are on the quarter system, you must, of course, adjust testing accordingly.

In most universities, the final examination is two or three hours long. It should follow the same general principle as the other tests—entirely in the target language, no translation, great emphasis on composition in various forms.

Oral Tests

Oral testing has two aspects. You will want to test the student's ability to take dictation, to understand a text, and to show his understanding by answering a series of true-false or multiple-choice questions. This is the more passive, more strictly "audio" part of oral testing. There is no better way to administer this sort of test than by using the laboratory.

Conversation

Although testing tapes will enable you to examine effectively the student's automatic responses, his ability to follow an oral text, to take dictation, and to answer questions correctly, you may also want to test the manner in which he can converse when face to face with a person. I do not think the laboratory is the best instrument for this sort of testing. I have never heard anyone have a lively or stimulating conversation with a machine. Here you need the live situation. In the Preface to the teachers in *Parole et Pensée* I have outlined a practical procedure for this kind of conversation testing. I will repeat it here briefly.

A few days ahead of the testing date make a schedule by which you arrange for two instructors, in addition to the regular classroom instructor, to be present at each class. Prepare a number of questions on slips of paper, as many and as varied as possible. Each instructor will receive a set of these questions in an envelope. On the day of the test, the students of each class are divided (alphabetically or otherwise) into three groups. Each instructor will examine one group. Each student draws a question—or two, from which he can choose—prepares it for two or three minutes, sits down with an instructor and converses with him for a few minutes. Table 3 gives an example of this type of discussion. I do not think it terribly important to hold the student to the specific question he has drawn. It should serve mostly as a point of departure. Ask questions, interrupt, help perhaps, elicit all possible conversation from him. Grade him on fluency, pronunciation, correctness of expression, and richness of vocabulary. Grades may then be handed to the regular classroom instructor, who will use them to prepare his composite oral grade for each student.

Tediously outlining every technique I recommend would be inappropriately burdensome for our present objective in this book. Hence, my emphasis on the method, its underlying principles, and some general procedures. The inclusion in some detail of certain techniques—such as writing, oral composition, presentation of readings—is intended to have been illustrative and not exhaustive. Similarly, the following chapters will indicate how language teachers at both college

Table 3. An Example of an Oral Examination*

PROFESSEUR: Alors, Mademoiselle, écoutez-vous la radio?

ETUDIANTE: Oui, Madame, j'écoute la radio souvent.

PROFESSEUR: Tous les jours?

ETUDIANTE: Oui, Madame, tous les jours parce que je vais à l'université dans moi voi... mon voi... ture, ma voiture.

PROFESSEUR: Ah oui?

ETUDIANTE: Et j'ai une radio dans la voiture.

PROFESSEUR: Très bien. Alors c'est très pratique?

ETUDIANTE: Oui.

PROFESSEUR: Vous écoutez les nouvelles dans votre voiture?

ETUDIANTE: Oui.

PROFESSEUR: Vous écoutez les nouvelles... mais qu'est-ce que vous écoutez encore à la radio?

ETUDIANTE: J'écoute qu[e]... qu[e] passe... qu[e] passe en... dans le monde.

PROFESSEUR: Les événements... dans le monde?

ETUDIANTE: Oui.

PROFESSEUR: La politique?

ETUDIANTE: Oui, mais j'écoute le jazz et la musique aussi. J'aime la musique.

PROFESSEUR: Bon, très bien. La musique... folklorique? La musique... classique? Quelle musique... préférez-vous?

ETUDIANTE: J'aim[ɛ̃]... j'aim[ɛ̃]... toute... la musique.

PROFESSEUR: Oh, mais c'est merveilleux! Vous n'avez pas de difficultés alors?

ETUDIANTE: Non... je n'ai [ə] pas de difficultés...

PROFESSEUR: Mais c'est très bien.

ETUDIANTE: Avec la musique.

PROFESSEUR: Si un jeune homme aime... la musique de jazz...?

ETUDIANTE: J'aime la musique de jazz aussi!

PROFESSEUR: C'est magnifique, n'est-ce pas? Bon. Alors, regardez-vous la télévision?

ETUDIANTE: Je... je regarde la télévision quelquefois mais je ne regarde pas souvent parce que j'ai beaucoup de travail.

PROFESSEUR: Ah oui? Vous avez beaucoup de travail . . . malheureusement?

ETUDIANTE: Non!

PROFESSEUR: Ah?

ETUDIANTE: Je... je suis... je suis enchantée avec mon travail.

PROFESSEUR: Bien.

ETUDIANTE: Parce que j'ai beaucoup... d' "intéresses."

PROFESSEUR: D'intérêts.

ETUDIANTE: D'intérêts.

PROFESSEUR: Oui!

ETUDIANTE: Dans mon travail.

PROFESSEUR: Alors c'est une très bonne chose d'avoir un travail très intéressant.

ETUDIANTE: Oui...

---

*Excerpt from an oral examination recorded in August, 1964, at Stanford. The student had been taking French for only eight weeks in a class using a preliminary version of *Parole et Pensée*. The question the student chose was: *"Préférez-vous écouter la radio, regarder la télévision ou lire le journal? Pourquoi?"* The oral examination was graded "B."

---

and secondary level have approached the problem of defining language teaching and how they have gone from the theory to the practice of the method. An item-by-item discussion of the specifics for teaching French grammar can be found in my textbooks and teacher's guides.

All of us who have practiced the verbal-active method have found a wide range of techniques and procedures, too numerous to inventory here, but still in complete harmony with the fundamental methodological precepts we propose for consideration. Of all educational processes, learning a language is perhaps the most truly educational, in the literal sense of *educere*, to bring out, to draw forth. Far from being a random process, it is, on the contrary, a rigorous one, subjected to laws not unlike those which govern organic growth. I have often compared it to the growth of a tree, with roots and branches seen as structures—means of support for leaves and flowers—even as sentence structure supports vocabulary. In this view, lists of disconnected words, recitation of verb forms, or memorization of dialogues, are no more viable than leaves, heaped on the ground in the hope of producing a tree. These would soon wither and no growth would take place. If instead, from a single but firm root a few healthy branches grow, these will support a few leaves. No matter how small, the tree will grow if it is viable. Thus, as basic structures are established, they become roots and branches capable of supporting a constantly growing and differentiating vocabulary. At all phases of learning there is a strong, healthy organism, systematically building upon itself. Language is alive, it possesses all the qualities of life itself, and its learning can only be a process of combined order and dynamism.

Notes

1. Much of what I have said here can also be found in my textbooks, *Parole et Pensée, Parole et Pensée du Professeur* (Harper & Row, 1965), *Teacher's Edition of Jeunes Voix, Jeunes Visages* (Harper & Row, 1970).

3

Ralph M. Hester

DIRECT METHOD EXPERIENCES
AT COLLEGE AND UNIVERSITY LEVEL

PRACTICING a rationalist direct method in foreign language teaching at college level will have innumerable implications, for the department concerned—in both its language and literature courses—and, naturally, for the undergraduate student, regardless of whether he attends a large university or a small college, and regardless of whether he is a foreign language major or not. The effects of a method, however great or small, will generally appear self-evident to teachers and students alike, who all too often feel little need for further enlightenment on the portent of any particular theory. Professors of foreign languages and literature are by definition a special class, but in judging language methodology they are usually quite satisfied that their experience was a good one, without taking into account their particular attitude and motivation. Besides, they are largely correct in assuming their way of having learned a foreign language would still be valid for the foreign language major, who, in turn, probably possesses an exceptional predisposition for acquiring another language. Foreign language majors are not, in fact, greatly interested in methodology, since their abilities carry them along at a rapid pace corresponding to their interest in the foreign language. We all know talented majors who by some psycho-linguistic miracle are amazingly proficient in spite of their background. The non-major, on the other hand, is usually meeting a requirement and will unquestioningly bear the prescribed courses without interrogating himself, the teacher, or the department, on the validity of the principle that determines the nature of the course. (He may, of course, be vociferous about content and techniques.) Nevertheless, it is undoubtedly the undergraduate non-major for whom the implications of a method are greatest.

Strictly as a question of numbers, the extent of a method's effects is clear: hundreds of thousands study foreign languages, few specialize in them. We shall hardly neglect the foreign language major in our discussion here, but there are many reasons that warrant priority to the non-specialist. Most foreign language departments and teachers spend the greater part of their effort, time, and budget teaching him, and yet so many of us remain no more than resigned to the democratization of education, perhaps feeling all the while that we are really an elite and that only an elite can attain any achievement in our field. Hence, our indulgence for the "ungifted language-learner" (half of our students?—probably 80 percent?). Yet quite independent of our opinion of the general college curriculum, we face the fact that we shall probably always teach students whose interest in foreign language in the great majority of cases is secondary at very best. How many language teachers have already dissertated about this situation without realizing that foreign languages are not an isolated case in any undergraduate program of general requirements! Moreover, what we should realize is that— contrary to the false assumption that foreign languages are particularly difficult—foreign languages are accessible to nearly everyone, and the foreign language teacher actually has an advantage over teachers of other disciplines in producing concrete results of learning. Exploiting this advantage is immeasurably beneficial to the undergraduate non-major, most satisfying to the teacher, and certainly facilitates a department teaching great numbers of students apprehensive or indifferent about what they consider the probably futile task of acquiring or trying to acquire a "special skill."

We can say without the slightest reservation that teaching a foreign language with a rationalist direct method will enable the non-specialist to achieve unusual competence, and,— perhaps in many ways more important—enable him to be aware of the fact that he has achieved competence! The teacher is always moved and encouraged by evidence of learning, but much learning takes place without the student being cognizant of its nature. What could be more rewarding to the teacher than observing that not only has learning occurred but that the learner is exulting in the experience because he understands why—even if only partially—or anticipates its possibilities. This is precisely what happens with a direct method practiced at college level. And it happens frequently, even constantly, in the classroom, to the extent that the non-major, unlike the major, becomes curious about foreign language teaching methodology. We have conducted special lectures and seminars for the general foreign language student simply interested in finding an explanation to his surprise: "How could I really be learning a foreign language when I thought it wasn't possible?"

One might reply that a student can have a feeling of accomplishment with any method. He, for example, who has memorized his dialogue, is proud to recite it correctly. But we believe that the element of surprise is lacking in this student's satisfaction, which can only come with a not entirely expected discovery: that he can express himself in a foreign language and not quite in the way he imagined. This is a fundamental point. The astonishment at finding an instrument that was there all the time is not unlike some definitions of poetry— Cocteau's, for example—and, for that matter, is related to that intellectual excitement of which Chomsky speaks, which precedes discovery when we manage to make phenomena "strange to ourselves."[1] We maintain that even the dullest individuals are capable of feeling the joy of invention when they speak. Written or spoken expression is indeed creativeness, and a student learning a foreign language with a method which assumes that the excitement of this originality is available to all, will indeed succeed in acquiring the target language.

I have deliberately spoken first of this crucial psychological assumption. If teachers, colleagues, and students cannot be convinced to accept it, even provisionally, until they see or participate in the concrete results of the method, then all the practical matters we discuss will seem scarcely pertinent. A rationalist direct method involves enough difficulty, especially in competition with the "smoothness" of audio-lingual methods, without constantly having to stir up belief and confidence in a principle to which few professors could normally adhere, namely that *all* students can be creative in their language and that foreign language is the ideal discipline in which to demonstrate this. Once the teaching staff is willing to experiment, it is immediately confronted with a variety of apparent obstacles, again, relatively speaking, for audio-lingual methods present many practical advantages. For example, teachers need not speak fluently the target language. The contingencies of immediate classroom reality are not a problem. The individual personality of the student is not a factor, since memorization and drill of models imposed from the outside are the reality. There is little to "discover," for everything is already explicit. A step-by-step sequence is simple to follow from the first level on. There is no multiple approach in teaching language skills to dose out in vaguely defined and simultaneous proportions. One can be concerned with one skill at a time. Students need not be introduced to grammatical reasoning since these concepts are not usually taught per se at secondary level English. The language laboratory is a convenient logical extension of classroom work with audio-lingual methods. For the experimenter, teaching machines and computer learning appear fraught with interest and promise. A plethora of material is available in texts, tests, method books, etc. A structural linguist has taught at nearly every NDEA institute for foreign language teachers, and most language consultants are audio-lingual experts. The composition of tests and quizzes is relatively easy since few responses are possible, so correction time is minimal. Little time is "wasted" in free give-and-take conversation or in free composition correction—oral or written—in the target language. And, finally, there is at least some testing evidence to indicate the superiority of audio-lingual methods over the old grammar-translation method.

The degree to which these advantages might deter experimentation with other methods, varies, of course, considerably according to the level, secondary or college. At any level, grammar-translation-reading methods may be practiced with the greatest facility because they are no method at all. Any teacher could be a foreign language teacher if he could keep his students sufficiently book-oriented. Audio-lingual methods mark a departure from this tradition, but still not enough of one. It is amazing with what efficiency structuralist theory and practice came to displace the linguistic eclecticism that underlay the mass of textbooks available, say, fifteen years ago. Just as many texts are available today, but they display a remarkable conformity in their material, the variance generally arising from the extent of concessions made to grammar-translation in compromising with audio-lingual approaches. I doubt a rationalist direct method could ever be extended over the country with such speed, since a certain amount of human inefficiency, I dare say, is a part of its precepts. A direct method is reality-(student-student-teacher-classroom) oriented with all the margin of possible confusion that this implies.

We have said that the teacher need not have high competence in the target language with an audio-lingual method, implying that he must with a direct method. However, this should not be seen as a stumbling block. Although by and large foreign language teachers of today do have adequate competence, it is a well-known fact that many teachers with only mediocre fluency can perform satisfactorily by diligent preparation and by keeping the learning pace within the strict confines of the lesson unit. With a direct method, because the learning dosage in all likelihood will go beyond the limits defined by chapter or section, linguistic competence is obviously indispensable. But this does not require native fluency. After all, the competent non-native instructor participates in the phenomenon of language invention just as his students do. The teacher of French, whose native language is English, is generally more apt than the Frenchman at finding, for example, cognate words and paraphrases that facilitate comprehension in the beginning while maintaining all communication in French. I know that some teachers, especially native speakers, might question certain "inventions" in the language of non-native speakers; but I have yet to find any student seriously misdirected by an imaginative semantic or phraseological solution to an unexpected teaching problem, as long as the solution remains grammatically conceivable and is clear, even though its usage is infrequent or without precedent. The beginning teacher in the beginning class is not to be condemned for saying *c'est similaire* rather than *pareil* or *c'est possible* rather than *peut-être*, because such examples mark passive transitions of simple listening-comprehension into more complex understanding. The student should not be drilled on *c'est possible*, but if he says it, the teacher should not discourage him with an inopportune correction. The student who understands *c'est possible* will in due time say *peut-être*. Even in the realm of pronunciation the principle is similar. The very fluent teacher will say *vous venez demain ou samedi* [vu vne dmɛ̃ u samdi], and the less fluent perhaps [vu vəne dəmɛ̃ u sa)mədi]. The less fluent teacher might even be intentionally including normally unpronounced mute *e*'s if he is over-articulating in his effort to be clearly understood. Again, the student who pronounces [vu vəne dəmɛ̃ u samədi] will, in due time, understand and reproduce [vu vne dmɛ̃ u samdi].

The question of competence and fluency is naturally much more complex. We simply wish to note here that a margin of imperfection is allowable. The experience of the beginning teacher, particularly the teaching assistant in a university, may often be very limited; his fluency in the target language may be evolving rapidly but he still remains far from perfection. He may nevertheless be a far better teacher of language than the native professor. We shall return to this question later in discussing the guidance necessary to a young teacher. In any case, there is little doubt that a direct method succeeds well when the teacher, on his level, is capable of evolving too. The dynamism of discovery and learning is all the more efficacious when it operates at both ends of the teacher-student exchange.

The force of this social psycho-linguistic phenomenon bears its finest fruit in terms of classroom reality, the common denominator which conducts individual student reality through multiple cross-currents in the spontaneity of self-expression. We have said that the contingencies of the classroom situation are not a problem with an audio-lingual method, since the material to be presented can be foreseen and prepared. On the other hand, a willingness to accept these uncertainties and an ever-improving effort to benefit from them, are fundamental sources of learning with a direct method, not to mention that delight and satisfaction, of which we spoke above, that come to teacher and student alike. Given the wonderment created by spontaneous invention and learning, contingency is hardly a "problem" at all. I recall a beginning class in which the teacher was collecting the first written homework without realizing the university bookstore had sold out its supply of texts and many students had no books. A resourceful student, never questioning his inability to express fully in French at the end of ten days all the subtleties of his frustration, triumphed over the situation by declaring "*Mais, monsieur, le livre est absent!*" This inventive exploitation of the few language tools he possessed resulted in a community sigh of relief, amusement at the teacher's surprise at this information, and then finally general satisfaction and wonderment that the communication had been effected within the rules of the game, that is, entirely in the target language. This "problem" of contingency thus solved itself. The example is not an isolated incident; it is the very objective of our method. Admittedly, other questions arise that are less easily or less spontaneously answered, but one can certainly learn to deal with the unexpected in the foreign language classroom.

The same can be said of the personality of a student. With an audio-lingual method this presents no hurdle for the teacher seeking to condition responses that have no relevance to him. Why encourage difficulties by being concerned with what Joe really does after class if (1) the dialogue to be memorized already states what the speakers do, or (2) a clarification of Joe's activities is likely to introduce constructions and vocabulary better delayed until a later unit (if by statistical miracle the vocabulary Joe needs is in the book)? Moreover, why force the not infrequently timid foreign language student to reveal things about himself that he would not want to discuss in the first place? The answer to this last question is to be found in the way in which the classroom reality is organized (or invented . . . or discovered) by the teacher.

This situation may, of course, be very artificial (in any other context there would be no reason for teacher and student ever to communicate in the target language), but it is a pedagogical fact that somehow, in some way, every student wants to discuss himself and be heard. A direct method provides an outlet for this basic psychological thrust. Naturally, the teacher may not be the least interested in what Joe actually does after class. But if the instructor is striving to achieve concrete results from his teaching, he will find there is much more to be gained in asking Joe what he really does than in merely confirming that Joe has correctly repeated what the dialogue says Jim does. We are not suggesting that one can systematically teach material drawn from an individual student's interest and personality, but the instructor should be alert and disposed to using and pedagogically benefiting from each student's personal contribution.

Obviously a core of subject matter exists of probably mutual interest to any class, as would be true of any social assembly constituted by common factors. Even certain of the most traditional texts (and especially their revised editions) show an attempt to interest students by including readings, dialogues and examples that are rich in contemporaneity hopefully pertinent to young people's lives. Audio-lingual texts reveal the same technique, but constant revision for present-day reality with all its fads and fancies is not feasible. Professors of foreign literatures not involved in language teaching have only the greatest of scorn for texts whose intellectual content seems as shallow as the superficial and evolving modes being discussed. Such scorn is not warranted when there are good pedagogical reasons, yet critics may be justified in pointing out how outdated the subject areas of some texts are after only three or four years. These things cannot be synchronized with a text.

A teacher may occasionally adapt textbook material by rewriting readings and dialogues to cover subjects particularly relevant to his students, while retaining the essential constructions and vocabularly of the original text. This represents quite an exercise in linguistic and stylistic artifice. It also takes considerable time, especially when the rewritten material must be reproduced or even recorded. My admiration knows no bounds for young teachers whom I have seen spending hours in literally composing new textbooks in their effort to render certain audio-lingual dialogues interesting and pertinent. Even with the given readings of a direct method text, instructors often revise the material to suit their students—again, still retaining essential constructions and vocabulary—or simply to present new vocabulary and expressions without reciting the reading in its exact order, so that the actual reading experience for the student will be at once new and familiar.

Is the teaching of grammar an unnecessary obstacle? Again, the difficulties here are diminished by any method based strictly on the notion of reflex conditioning, mimicry, and memorization. Audio-lingual methods may, of course, explain grammar, but explanations are still kept to a minimum, and the possibility of grammatical reasoning remains unemphasized. Students thus taught may "perform" well without ever achieving a real operational mode functioning in all situations through the generative potential of grammar. I shall not insist further here upon the role of grammar in a rationalist direct method. That has been made clear in the first chapter of this book. Nevertheless, a reply must be given to the exasperated college foreign language instructor who would welcome a structuralist method because it avoids his having to teach what he feels the secondary school should have taught in the first place. Some years ago, the professional journals were full of advice to foreign language teachers on how to teach grammar, something apparently not taught in English classes, and these articles often did not hide their reproach to instructors of English. As a matter of fact, these same criticisms are still heard —if not printed—in some college departments. English, of course, has been subject not only to the laicization of education, just as foreign language has, but English grammar as a subject area presents peculiar difficulties to the average student which, in fact, the foreign language does not. We all know that the grammaticalness of English is simply not as obvious as in the other less evolved languages which most of us teach. Similarly, we know students who declare they never really understood English until they learned German or Latin. Unfortunately, what we suspect is true concerning this claim remains difficult to prove. What is true is that the difficulty of teaching English grammar to English-speaking students—or the so-called failure of secondary schools to accomplish as much—does not determine the difficulty of teaching foreign language grammar. One might say it is a facility rather than a difficulty. Foreign language grammars lend themselves to the teaching of grammar. This is not to say there are no thorny areas; there are. Many of them derive from the obscurity of English grammar, and the problem of transference, but this does not warrant our generalizing about the grammatical inaptitude of our students. Their errors lie much more frequently in striking details than in syntactical concepts. Forgetting a root form, an ending, an agreement, or using the wrong preposition or the wrong case are mistakes to be expected. The student who cannot understand what an agreement, a preposition, or a case is deserves special attention, for he is very rare, and practically nonexistent at college level. Some students may learn a foreign language only with great difficulty, but their difficulty is not explained simply by their inability to understand the deep and abstract concepts of grammar. On the contrary, the capacity within them to understand these concepts may assist them immensely.

We do not, in a direct method, teach grammar with the objective that students should be trained in grammatical analysis. Quite the opposite. Deductive learning is the basis of most of our techniques. We believe, however, that an awareness of grammar not only satisfies the normal intellectual curiosity of the college learner but that understanding it helps him to learn more easily by deduction each ensuing step. Actually, in the beginning we try to circumvent too many grammatical explanations, since we prefer to use our class time in meaningful practice and in inculcating spontaneity rather than bogging down in grammatical descriptions. The dosage of grammar and the degree of explanation have already been discussed. I emphasize here only the necessity and facility of teaching grammar to college students of foreign language.

Even though a step-by-step sequence emphasizing one skill at a time appears logical and easy to follow for both teacher and student, there is no conclusive evidence proving that these assumptions are pedagogically valid. Again, it is not my intention to dwell at lenth on the psycho-linguistic principles that justify a multiple approach, since this is already argued effectively elsewhere by de Sauzé and his current followers. The appropriateness of a multiple approach at college level seems compelling. It is true that in the beginning there must be some exclusive concentration on listening-comprehension, not only to accustom the student to the sounds of the new language and the understanding resulting from their association with meaningful practice, but to stimulate the whole aural faculty, which is generally not fully exploited in the learning process at school. This has become a truism in language teaching. However, the priority accorded the ear and then, soon thereafter, oral expression, should not preclude the eye, since the visual faculty is normally the dominant faculty, both in learning and in reinforcement. Reading and writing can and should—even at an early stage—accompany listening and speaking. Writing, especially, is as much a part of language creation—even if at a different level—as is speaking, and should, we believe, precede and then accompany the practice of serious reading.

Listening-understanding, speaking, writing, and reading remain, for us, largely concomitant activities as we proceed from the simple and basic to the complex and decorative, emphasizing one grammatical problem at a time and continually reinforcing it as it becomes integrated into the whole language learning and practice process. We use a new word, form, or structure in a context relevant to the classroom-student reality, we render it immediately understandable by any one of various combined techniques (analogy and contrast—synonym, antonym—definition in simple or cognate terms, description, illustration, acting out, etc.); then we propose it as a subject for discussion in elementary question-answer form. Once the new form has been used by a majority of the class, individually or in unison, we seek to induce a deduction of the rule by the students, helping them to express their understanding by providing these terms: *adjectif, après, avant, avec, parce que, quand, si, féminin, masculin*. The student has understood as of the first week that *he* must express himself in complete sentences and it is his problem to formulate a rule within his linguistic limits: *"Pourquoi 'un'?"*... *"Parce que cahier est masculin."* If he does not succeed, we finally formulate the rule and provide him with another example calling for the same explanation: *"Pourquoi 'un' crayon?"*

It is obvious that the actual discussion of grammar becomes, at times, a part of the classroom "reality" to which we have referred. Consideration of a *cahier sur une chaise* will momentarily attract attention if the teacher singles out the object, but asking *why un* or *une* will prolong attention and create interest. The force of *why* is ever-present, since the student conditioned to communication in a foreign language is already conditioned to a certain effort of understanding which begs to be relieved: the sound and the meaning are grasped . . . now *why* the particular form? Of course this is true of any learner, consciously or unconsciously, but the impact of intellectual curiosity is proportional to intellectual capacity and training, which can practically be reduced to a question of age, at least as far as grammatical logic is concerned. The child learning a foreign language is content merely to imitate, since he generally accepts a foreign language as a kind of absolute truth, just as he does his own language. Not so with the adolescent, whose reasoning ability, as we all know, seeks to exercise itself. This is true of the young teenager (which will be discussed in the last chapter of this book); it is strikingly true of the college student. Although we proceed to study grammar piecemeal, we aim, in the end, to meet the expectations of the student to possess on an abstract level the inner-workings of the foreign linguistic system. And for all the complex simultaneity that this procedure involves, we meet the expectations through understanding, speaking, and writing all at once.

After a grammatical rule is deduced and formulated in class, it can be applied in writing immediately—original sentences written on the board, written exercises, short compositions, dictations—and then as written homework. Reinforcement of the learned material then occurs in an elementary form of reading: recognition on the printed page of the rules and examples, sentences and explanations, already presented and formulated in class, and the illustration of new vocabulary and structure in a simple reading text. The text is, of course, presented by the instructor to the students in class before they see ("read") it. Subsequent oral and written work can then be based on the reading, before the presentation of another problem begins. A usual order would then be: *listening-understanding, speaking-writing-reading-speaking-writing*. This is what we understand by a multiple approach within a single unit.

Another reason for a multiple approach can be found in the general boredom that overcomes the student in the language laboratory once he has abandoned his original enthusiastic assumption that he could learn a foreign language largely passively through the miracle of the machine, by sound, imitation, and repetition. The laboratory is indeed a logical extension of structuralist concepts, as most laboratory programs will reveal in the dominance of mimicry and transformation-type drills. In our opinion, these exercises may well have a certain usefulness, but they should not take up the entire laboratory program. The hearing of a dialogue in the laboratory followed immediately by recorded drill on its structures is not a valid point of departure. The use and misuse of laboratories has become a vast area of professional criticism constituting an awesome bibliography in a relatively short time. Here I wish to mention only certain areas of the laboratory problem basic to our method.

First of all, the laboratory is certainly compatible with a direct method. As mentioned above, drill and some repetition of structures can help learning . . . provided that they are conceived as more supplementary than complementary to classroom learning. We do not believe that laboratory presentation of new structures can be the proper medium for inducing learning. The laboratory should serve as a possible medium of reinforcement, and, especially at college level, where there are fewer problems of administration, discipline, and overseeing of expensive and delicate equipment, the laboratory should allow the student to do what he may not be able to do in class—reinforce learning at his own pace.

Wherever possible, laboratories should be operated on a library-type basis. The variance of individual capacities of concentration, limited to the auditory faculty, is infinite. The value of a class period, where all faculties are operative in learning, far outweigh that of an equal laboratory period. If a library system of laboratory operation is impossible, then we recommend laboratory equipment that allows the student to work individually at his own pace within the class laboratory hour. This naturally complicates the role of the monitor who could otherwise listen to any student at any time and know exactly what to anticipate. However, the smoothness of the laboratory operation in terms of monitor efficiency is not a criterion. An unmonitored student may not be so much the victim of mislearning as he is of no learning at all. Yet a laboratory must be monitored, since there is now ample proof to show that only a small proportion of foreign language students working alone with solely recorded material are able to (1) recognize an erroneous variant, and (2) correct it. This is most obvious in the case of pronunciation, where seeing and even feeling may be often indispensable to correction and improvement.

The recorded laboratory program should include exercises for review of structures, vocabulary, and sounds already covered in class, but it should present the materials in a more varied format than is generally done. More listening-comprehension type exercises should be given, since this is the indisputable domain of aural learning, and the laboratory can offer a variety of voices, which the teacher cannot. Furthermore, the student should be allowed to answer questions both orally and in writing. Then, either based on the listening-comprehension recording, or perhaps on the reading of the current lesson in the textbook, "free" questions should be included in an exercise in which there are many ways of answering correctly. The monitor or the instructor may not have the possibility of correcting every student's response, but we feel that the possibility of variance—the trial and error of language invention—must be to some extent translated from the classroom into the laboratory. Uncorrected incorrectness is not to be feared as much as the banning of originality and the mistakes it entails.

Laboratory programs should also include dictations, without by any means excluding them from class, in spite of all that has been said about eliminating them from both class and laboratory. In a direct multiple-approach method, the dictation is the perfect alliance of listening-comprehension and writing. Again, in a dictation, the laboratory can provide a variety of voices. However, in class, comprehension generally results in part from the student seeing the reader of the dictation speak and gesture, so that a laboratory dictation is partially false in the same way all laboratory work is unauthentic: one does not communicate in normal language with a machine.

The machine has proved to be an impasse. Laboratories, recorded programs, machine learning, translators, and computers have a certain usefulness in foreign language study, but their potential application is obviously much less promising than was originally believed. "Pure" informative prose, for example, can be translated by machines, but the impossibility of automatic translation of normal language, with its infinite variety of decorative confusion arising from the depths of the mind, contributed to the revolt against the limits of structural descriptive linguistics. We believe a direct multiple-approach method in the teaching of foreign language to be extraordinarily in harmony with the start of a new era in general language study, still in an embryonic stage.

Consequently, there are not as yet great numbers of linguistic theorists concerned with foreign language teaching based on the hypotheses of generative grammar. Neither are there many textbooks other than those mentioned in the introduction; and foreign language consultants, unfortunately, are not familiar with them. *Parole et Pensée,* of course, is a widely used college text, but apparently the principles underlying it are not yet fully appreciated or contrasted with those of other methods.[2] This situation is normal. One era of any discipline does not evolve into a new era with one spurt. As a new trend in language teaching begins to take on a clearer form, we shall rediscover the de Sauzé of fifty years ago, just as Chomsky and contemporary linguists have rediscovered the Wilhelm von Humboldt and the Port Royal grammarians of previous centuries. Within this decade we are certain to see an increasing number of beginning foreign language textbooks resulting from new theories of linguistics and psychology, and, hopefully, more psycho-linguists in foreign language institutes to link the new school of thought with its practical application for the teacher.

Up to now, the teacher attending an NDEA institute has usually found at least one structuralist expert explaining the theory from which the audio-lingual method has been derived. This staffing procedure was to be expected. In view of the types of texts available and the quantities in which they were published and purchased, a descriptive linguist was a logical and efficient choice. This situation will undoubtedly change, just as the efficiency of the audio-lingual method will give way to another kind of efficiency. For example, the multiple-choice blank-completion test, however much time it saves the teacher, is now quite open to question. "How many times," recently asked a psycho-linguist, "have you 'filled in a blank' when formulating what you wanted to say?" It is not unreasonable to predict that original composition, oral or written, will become a much more widely used device of learning and evaluation in the teaching of foreign languages, just as it may in the teaching of literature. If available correction time is extremely limited, then a strict limit on the length of compositions must be imposed. A five-sentence composition may well have more value than an exercise with fifty blanks. Short exercises in vocabulary and structure are not to be banished from the learning process in class any more than they are in the laboratory, but they should probably play an increasingly reduced role.

The good teacher is naturally concerned about efficient use of time—his, his students, and that of the class as a whole. The use of English, for example, would assure faster communication and comprehension when difficult abstract grammatical concepts are discussed, or limiting practice to a single structure or a well-defined pattern, which would undeniably reduce the expenditure of psycho-linguistic energy. Mimicry, likewise, requires barely the slightest interval of time between the given model and its reproduction. Correction is immediate. The recitation of a memorized dialogue is usually fast and impressive. Our objection is, however, that all these time-saving devices may be ineffectual in learning the language. Strict pattern drill very definitely is inefficacious if one accepts the premise that language is invention. We have often spoken of meaningful practice, whereas this practice often has an apparent but superficial aspect of disorder. The instructor must guide the student into using the form being taught in his own way: *"Où est la clé de votre auto?"*—*"elle est dans ma poche."* Immediately supplying *"elle est dans ma poche"* to be repeated would be a rapid way to cover a personal pronoun problem and would even have the appearance of being "personal." *(La clé de l'auto d'un étudiant est probablement dans sa poche!)* However, the beginning student who is allowed a slight pause for the whole cerebral process to produce an answer, or the student who stumbles through *"La clé de ma auto . . . de mon auto... elle... elle... est sur le bureau... dans mon... ma chambre"* has undoubtedly acquired an operative language tool of wider application than he who has only to repeat a possibly meaningful response. There is much order in the apparent disorder of direct method practice. Although we do not know yet what this order is, we are convinced that it is very clearly ordered. We are not "wasting" time in meaningful practice, we are gaining it.

In saying that we do not know what this order is, we are not announcing a new mystery, nor are we disclaiming the testability of our method. We are only echoing the statements of current researchers in language and linguistics who avow the inadequacy of current understanding. Comparing audio-lingual methods with the old grammar-translation-reading method was a fairly easy testing problem. There exists evidence to indicate the superiority of the former, in that the New Key produces students who have a higher proficiency in understanding the spoken language and in pronouncing it. This audio-lingual achievement is accompanied by less certain advantages in reading and writing (we do not mean "writing" by filling in blanks here), yet a direct method trained student shows the same superior achievement. There are not as yet published test results comparing audio-lingual trained students with students trained in a rational direct method as we understand it.[3] This is still another area awaiting research. A recent study conducted at Purdue University between an audio-lingual Spanish text and a "cognitive-code" text gave results favoring the cognitive-code theory (by the slightest margin), but the most significant conclusion of the study was its formulation of testing areas still unexplored.[4] Moreover, in our opinion, the choice of a so-called "cognitive-code" text was very misleading since it was in many ways a rather traditional text, with little or no systematic oral emphasis.

Those colleges and universities that have been using direct method texts have continued to do so during the past decade in ever-increasing numbers. Their satisfaction with the method arises largely from the intuitive conviction of their good teachers that impressive results are being obtained. Testing for immediate practical purposes has been conducted, of course, but not for research purposes or publication. Moreover, testing has often been done with standardized national tests, which, in fact, are generally intended for either the traditionally trained or the audio-lingual trained student. It is worth noting that the direct method trained student performs with high achievement on either kind of test. A glance at the adoption lists of publishers of direct method texts indicates that schools who have once used a direct method only rarely ever change to an audio-lingual method.

We must point out that foreign language departments using direct method texts achieve maximum results under certain conditions that warrant some discussion. For example, as with any method calling for frequent use of the foreign language, a direct method requires that a class not be too large. Twelve to sixteen has been said to be an ideal number of students but with a direct method, it should perhaps not be this small. Certainly satisfactory results may be obtained in a college foreign language class of twenty; twenty-five is difficult, but possible; beyond that, there are diminishing returns. Our recommending not too small a class requires some explanation, since foreign language teachers have often considered the fewer students the better the class. We believe that fifteen to twenty students are generally necessary for establishing an adequate social situation. Frequent communication and spontaneity occur naturally in a community composed of certain individual types (the prestigious, the well-known, the likeable, the attractive, the extrovert, the eloquent, the polemical, the ironical, etc.). We frankly confess that the statistical chances of succeeding with a direct method in a coeducational class of twenty are greater than in a class of ten timid girls, although we know the method has produced excellent results in small evening classes of adult engineers and classes of Air Force pilots stationed abroad.

The class must have a sense of community. The different personalities contributing to the total class personality may easily establish the feeling of community by unconscious mutual agreement, or it may be created by a good instructor who knows how to prod his students astutely into "playing the game." Likewise, the game must be played, and by "game" we mean not only the willingness with which students accept communication uniquely in the target language, but also the willingness with which they enter with the instructor into the elementary reality of the foreign language classroom. This is not an atmosphere full of subtleties; it may even be caricatural in its simplicity *(Mademoiselle Roberts est petite, blonde, et elle est gentille)*. Obviously this kind of uncomplicatedness, so necessary in the beginning, will eventually evolve. It is the teacher's responsibility to make certain everyone believes in the reality from the start. Outside of the classroom, Mademoiselle Roberts may be not infrequently hot-tempered, but students in the class will easily accept her with the pleasant character she apparently has most of the time. If this classroom personality is unbearably different from her true character for someone who knows her well, then the teacher should welcome her acquaintance's protest—if it comes—probably in the form of an ironical affirmation *(Oui... oui... Mademoiselle Roberts est gentille!")* or an outright negation *("Mademoiselle Roberts n'est pas gentille!")*, in which case the community will come to sense the complexity of Mademoiselle Roberts' nature without being able to express it in a psychological analysis *("Mademoiselle Roberts est gentille dans la classe, mais elle n'est pas gentille quand elle est avec Monsieur Hodge. C'est l'opinion de Monsieur Hodge.")*.

Even the timid student may be invited to play the game if the instructor gives him a characterization that he and the community will provisionally accept. *"Une maison?"* asks the instructor introducing the definite article as he sketches an ostentatious palace on the board. *"C'est un château... mais un château ordinaire?... non! c'est un château extraordinaire... c'est le château de Monsieur White!"* And so Monsieur White suddenly becomes the surprised and proud possessor of a castle, whereas in his timidity he might not speak of his house. His dwelling may then serve as a point of reference later on, for example, when the class learns he has several *châteaux*. Monsieur White could have also been encouraged to enter into his fictitious reality in the community by the teacher's renaming him "Monsieur Leblanc," a simple first-day-of-class act that confers enormous possibilities of self-realization upon the seed of the French classroom personality. Mademoiselle Horne could be transformed either into "Mademoiselle Corne" or "Mademoiselle" orn. In sum, whatever technique may be used, an hour-a-day community must be established in which every constituent will participate. The spirit of collaboration with which college foreign language students rapidly construct this reality is remarkable.

Naturally, much depends on the teacher who, as we said earlier, must, in a sense, evolve with the changing reality of the classroom; this is not always easy. A teacher who is open and sensitive to the actions and reactions of the students would have a pedagogical advantage in any discipline, but this kind of psychological trait cannot really be learned or acquired. Nothing, I should say, is easier than allowing and enabling a student to speak of *his* reality, as it is, as he sees it, as his peers see it, as he, or they, imagine or would like it to be. Creating the possibility of expressing this in a foreign language becomes the problem of a specific discipline. Again, the young teacher, competent and fluent in the foreign language, but who still has progress to make, is probably the ideal instructor. The accomplished, experienced, master teacher has undoubtedly stylized his attitudes and technique, at least to some extent, so that while possessing a definite pedagogical advantage, he may be—if only in some small way—less adaptable to an evolving reality than his neophyte apprentice. This question of openness would be of marginal importance in a field where only the transmission of knowledge is fundamental. In the foreign language classroom, we believe we should have as our first objective the creation of a constant language experience from which knowledge of the foreign language arises.

At large universities where a direct method is used,[5] demonstration classes taught by professors have guided younger teaching assistants. The latter, as nearly all practice teachers agree, gain infinitely more from seeing an excellent teacher perform than from reading or hearing about pedagogical techniques. Seeing an experienced teacher practicing a direct method is all the more important for the young language teacher, whose own foreign language learning experience may have been quite different. Under these circumstances, he can acquire the technique of the method as well as his colleague who has learned the language in this way. In general, teaching assistants are not only conscientious and enthusiastic, but adaptable and inventive, provided they are given a model and clearly defined principles to follow. There is undeniably a problem of regimentation within a large department language program when one method is prescribed while the beginning teacher wants to be original. (I'm sure that every enthusiastic young teacher at one time or another has wanted to write his own grammar book.) It seems to us, nevertheless, that no method offers so wide a margin for the individual teacher's techniques and so many possibilities for the development of his own teaching personality.

Intra-departmental collaboration in practicing the method is clearly an asset, particularly with respect to oral examinations. A single instructor's systematically administering all examinations to all his students is hardly feasible. The experienced instructor, needless to say, is usually quite capable of evaluating his students' oral performance from their class participation and oral compositions, just as he is probably able to estimate their overall performance in writing or reading without necessarily having recourse to an examination. Yet not providing for some oral control would be no different from eliminating tests in other areas. An oral examination (aided by others within the department) should, as all examinations, offer an objectivity not otherwise available, even though it may merely confirm the instructor's independent evaluation. This confirmation will satisfy both teacher and student. The examination should be pedagogical; again, both teacher and student should learn something from it. Perhaps the greatest value of an oral examination lies in its psychological impact upon the student, since oral timidity generally presents a problem for any language learner. In most cases, this timidity can be overcome with practice. The oral examination is then an intensification of that experience. In a test situation or in any situation where the only possibility would be to express oneself with difficulty in a new language, communication will require the summoning of a certain presence of mind sufficient to triumph over shyness and linguistic confusion.

We have applied these techniques of regularly administering oral examinations at mid-term and the end of the term in all first-year courses according to procedures suggested above by Mrs. Lenard. In some second-year college courses, all examinations have been given only at the end of the term, because of practical limitations. We have arranged for oral examinations by having two to four staff members individually test every student in a class during one period. This naturally requires that most language instructors give some extra time—two to four hours—during oral testing periods. It is advisable, moreover, to arrange the examination schedule so that the instructor will not be testing his own students. The reasons are obvious. The examiner has time to test some five to seven students in one class hour, and if they are from the examiner's own class then the possibility of an "objective" evaluation no longer exists.

The examination may be presented in several different ways. (See Table 3 on pp. 62–63 for one example.) Since the student would be provided with familiar subject matter, we feel he should be offered a choice of questions. The questions may be on separate slips of paper in an envelope from which he draws two or three and then chooses one. The examiner allows the student a moment or two to organize his thoughts. The student being tested may then speak on a subject which probably has already been discussed in class, e.g., *Ma famille*,

Mon actrice préférée, Un livre que j'aime, etc. The examiner then questions the student further to elicit responses likely to require certain structures emphasized during the term: *"Que faites vous après?... je fais... nous faisons. Est-ce que c'est vraiment une bonne actrice? Elle est meilleure que... elle est plus naturelle que... et elle est plus belle que...,"* etc. The question may include some grammatical requirements, such as *Faites des comparaisons avec... Utilisez des phrases telles que "Je suis content que... "* or *"Je n'aime pas que.... "*

Each examiner should be provided with a sheet of instructions indicating what to emphasize, because a teacher of only second-year courses may assist with first-year examinations. An evaluation sheet for the instructor should include general facility of oral expression, grammar, vocabulary, pronunciation, and specific remarks. It is extremely helpful to the student if the examiner also jots down for him in writing the mistakes and weaknesses noted during the test. The examiner must decide judiciously what proportion of mistakes to correct during the test and what proportion to indicate afterwards. Since the test lasts only five to ten minutes, delaying the greater part of the correction until the end is preferable. Linguistic "stage fright" presents enough difficulty without driving a student into silence or incoherence with corrections in rapid succession. While the examiners are testing in the classroom, students awaiting their turn may stay in the hall.

In second-year classes, we have found it often advisable to examine students in small groups of from three to five. The questions proposed may refer to more serious discussions derived from the readings in the text. Because consideration of a text is normally a community exchange of opinion, it is only appropriate that discussion should take place during a test in a group arrangement. The group agrees on the choice and is then allowed a few minutes to prepare. The examiner must make sure that each member of the group contributes to the discussion-test. One question could be *"Que pensez-vous de l'opinion de cet auteur à propos de l'armement militaire pour une guerre défensive?"*

The laboratory, too, may be used for some supplementary oral testing in listening-comprehension and dictation. It can offer an efficient way of testing for pronunciation improvement and evaluation of reading aloud provided there are means to correct the student's recording. Reading aloud from a text is a special aspect of pronunciation which we would rank low in skill priority for beginning language classes and can be partially treated in laboratory sessions. Only occasionally should it ever be a classroom activity in the teaching of reading or pronunciation, because it is hardly indispensable to either. Of course, reading aloud should not be neglected, but it is more a problem for phonetics or other advanced courses.

Another area of oral testing should be basic to any university foreign language program: the placement test. There would be no point in enumerating the difficulties which language departments create for themselves by not including an oral part in a placement test. Every college teacher knows that freshmen with the same number of years in a high school foreign language course may be nowhere so unequal in their skills as in oral expression. Recorded speaking tests, unfortunately, cannot always be graded as fast as is required by placement tests results. In lieu of a standardized recorded speaking test, we recommend a simple oral interview, somewhat similar to the oral examination. With a little experience, a department may develop a list of criteria and a simple format and evaluation sheet for the interviewer. There are admittedly numerous problems of scheduling and distribution of staff work loads in interviewing great numbers of freshmen. This is in addition to whatever other correction may be required by a placement test (listening-comprehension, reading, writing). The task can, nevertheless, be accomplished if the procedures are well organized. For example, over the past five years we have, at Stanford, placed an average of five hundred freshmen taking this type of placement test in French. The interviewing alone obviously demands the co-operation of every language instructor and staff member (taking appointments, interviewing, compiling results, etc.), but the results are indisputably worth the effort. All college teachers of beginning foreign language classes are aware of the number of non-beginners present. Equalizing the level of students within a single class beyond the first of a series of courses (e.g. French I or First-Year Beginning French) becomes more and more difficult as one progresses from the first to the second year. Ignoring the most active of language skills, oral expression, renders the problem not only difficult but insoluble, and, in fact, renders the whole placement undertaking quite ineffectual. The concerned second-year instructor has every right to complain about students proficient in only one or two skills. A student with unequal abilities who has already studied a foreign language for some time may progress in listening-comprehension, writing, and reading simply by following the chronological order of the college language courses offered, but if he is remarkably deficient in speaking, then it is doubtful he can improve without going back and acquiring some very basic oral skills in an earlier course.

Over the past decade most college professors of foreign languages and literatures have been pleasantly surprised by the increasing number of freshmen whose secondary school foreign language preparation has been sufficient to place him into the third and fourth-year courses. This number is not large compared to the total number of entering freshmen, but it is promising and certainly represents the generally improved status of foreign language teaching at the secondary level. Whatever the inadequacies of audio-lingual method, there is no doubt that the New Key came with an era of progress in foreign language teaching. Unfortunately, the increased number of students exposed to foreign language over longer periods of time at elementary and secondary levels has not resulted in greatly increased numbers of foreign language majors at college level, and certainly most foreign language majors do not begin their study of foreign language in college, at least with respect to those languages widely taught at pre-college level. The foreign language major is usually predisposed toward languages before he leaves high school, and in fact, has usually studied a foreign language at least two years before entering college. He is, again unfortunately, often the source of the third and fourth-year instructor's despair. The majors who actually begin their foreign language study at college are fewer in number, but, on the other hand, they are generally better students. I am not speaking, of course, of the rare brilliant student who may have years of foreign language study behind him. I would estimate that as a group those who started their foreign language at college have a 10 percent higher Grade Point Average than those who began in high school. There are no national statistics compiled from studies conducted over long periods of time in this area, so there is not as yet conclusive evidence. There are reasons to hope, however, that future studies and statistics will indicate the validity of our contention that one learns a language better in late adolescence than in late childhood.[6]

The college foreign language and literature professor may perhaps be extremely unhappy about his students' ability, but he should direct his criticism toward the probable source of his dissatisfaction. It is regrettable that college professors of foreign literature do not take a serious interest in furthering their profession by exploring its foundation, which is in the preparation of foreign language students at all levels. We have reason to believe that a rationalist direct method, like the verbal-active method, develops extraordinarily well both the average and the superior foreign language student, but we do not claim to be exempt from criticism. We recognize, for example, that we have colleagues who take a dim view of what they consider our permissive attitude toward mistakes in the beginning. They may disagree with our expressing a certain norm of the language (e.g., *le français quotidien*) apparently inferior to an absolute literary standard to which they subscribe. They say that using the target language exclusively is a fetish, that creativeness is merely a catchy phrase, that serious reading is delayed too long. Some feel that an effective teacher should be only a model and never a reality for the class, otherwise demagogy and fun result. They say that student reality at this level is not intellectually appropriate and is hardly subject matter for discussion; encouraging cleverness or cuteness in style is wrong; excellent pronunciation is not demanded enough, etc. Some of the criticisms concern only techniques, others touch at the basis of the method. In sum they come generally from critics who conceive of both language and literature as a special domain which the student must "acquire" more than "experience." We can only repeat our belief that not only is language a personal invention, but literature is as well, and the teaching of both language and literature should be more similar than they presently are.

We are still too much on the threshold of a new era in language theory and foreign language teaching to propose conclusive proof from testing here. Our assertions remain based both on the most recent linguistic hypothesis and on several years of promising experience at the hundreds of colleges and universities that have begun using a rationalist direct method of foreign language teaching. Audio-lingual methods, of course, have never succeeded through testing as much as through faith. A recent conference on the undergraduate major in French[7] expressed dissatisfaction with the state of things and called for a revision of goals and methods. The present situation was described as a battle between traditionalists and audio-lingualists—as if there were no other choice! "Male students, in particular, feel at a disadvantage with respect to girls whose talent for speech mimicry is generally greater than theirs."[8] However, in seeking ways to attract men students through intellectual challenge, the conference recommended a reform that would begin with a new heavy emphasis on reading including the art of reading texts aloud. We would agree that reading should eventually become the most serious ultimate goal of foreign language teaching, but to separate it so distinctly from other skills is simply acquiescing to the weaknesses of audio-lingual methods. All the skills should be taught all the time. True reading is admittedly the most difficult achievement, but divorcing it from writing, as the Colby Conference suggests, will most surely discourage the superior male student. To delay writing and stylistics —the most creative aspects of language learning—until graduate study is to neglect deliberately that which appeals most to the student really capable of involving himself in literature. How many times it has been said that the professor of literature is really an "écrivain manqué"! We furthermore highly question the statement that translation is the final step of understanding both in language and literature courses. What is meant by "understanding"? A passive reception of "pure" meaning? And even if this were partially possible with simple prose, what about poetry? What "understanding" is to be translated? We repeat our belief that one cannot understand if one cannot invent. Speaking and writing a language clearly require creativeness without translation.

Students themselves find most rewarding the experience of what they call "thinking in the foreign language." Although student evaluations hardly represent infallible judgments, they do often contain many elements of truth. At the University of California at Berkeley, where there are perhaps the most brutally critical of American college students, we find their assessment of a direct method—which obviously pertains to the "relevance" they are seeking (and which the Colby Conference noted as generally lacking in the French major)—to be extremely encouraging. Three months after the method was begun the Berkeley student *Slate-Supplement To The General Catalogue* included, amidst its stinging barbs, the following remarks:

The most spectacular reaction from students has come from those taking beginning French. Examples of this reaction include the comments: "The new method gets an 'A'." "I'm enjoying learning French." "No superlative can indicate how good this method really is . . ." A method by which grammar is picked up from speaking the language rather than by artificial memorization of rules. *Parole et Pensée*, the text used in French I, II, and III, is written in French and uses the conversational method.[9]

At the end of the year, student opinion continued to record that

The adoption of the conversational method in the teaching of beginning French has been a tremendous success over the past three quarters. According to students, the technique of holding the class entirely in French and requiring active oral participation makes the student learn to think in French. The text used in French I, II, and III, *Parole et Pensée* is considered excellent by students . . .[10]

And still a year later:

FRENCH I, II, III. "The basis of the new technique in French teaching here at Cal is that the student *thinks* in French rather than transposing from English to French." Often the instructor will speak nothing but French in class for the whole of the course. This tends to panic many students at first, but many are surprised at the facility with which they begin to pick up the language using this method.[11]

Furthermore, this kind of enthusiasm has been accompanied by some measurable results. At Stanford, for example, changes were instituted in the French major program, including teaching through a direct method in courses of the first two years. Whereas the student majoring in French had previously corresponded to the type noted by the Colby Conference, five years later the situation had been reversed. Within five years and with only a slight increase in the actual number of majors, the average GPA of all French majors had gone steadily up. More important, French had as high or higher a proportion of excellent students (3.4 GPA) than other departments of language and literature (26.9 percent).[12] Third-semester students at a nearby junior college using the same language teaching method surprised their teacher with an original one-act play in French which the class had decided to write on its own initiative. In different departments using the method, literary contests have appeared for first and second-year non-majors. Ninety percent of the contributions have been poems, and if the contributors are not great poets, they have nevertheless given evidence of a not inconsiderable language sensitivity. Very few of the authors have ever thought of composing poems in English, and it is, of course, interesting that their expression of originality should take place in French. A French I student at a state college composed the following poem:

LES FLEURS

Les fleurs grandissent
Verdissent, jaunissent
Bleuissent, embellissent.
Les fleurs brunissent
Palissent et vieillissent.[13]

We reaffirm our belief that the student encouraged to experiment creatively in the foreign language will prove to be the one who reacts most deeply and analytically to the literature of that language. A fifth-quarter student of French made this prose contribution to a *concours littéraire:*

DANS LES CHAMPS, LE DOUZE MARS

La pluie coule goutte à goutte entre vos épines.. C'est une sensation délicieuse, la sensation d'être un clavecin sous les mains d'un virtuose qui est en train de jouer une fugue bien compliquée de Bach. La terre s'harmonise et vos racines commencent à s'allonger en cherchant un sentier entre les petites roches et les morceaux de sol. Vos feuilles se réjouissent et vos fruits dansent dans la pluie. Vous êtes si heureux d'être un artichaut.[14]

It will be recalled that in the opening pages of this book, we quoted an analogy made between writing poetry and the learning of a foreign language, even in its most tedious grammatical aspects. To conclude, we return to that thought in a concrete form, poetically expressed by a third-quarter student:

GRAMMAIRE

Le féminin et masculin
Ainsi avec un verre de vin
Ont décidé d'être un
Se débarrasser des règles, demain.
Ils ont parlé de l'imparfait
Conditionnel, plus-que-parfait,
Et d'autres choses très compliquées.[15]

Notes

1. Chomsky, *Language and Mind* p. 52.
2. Ann Gut, "Programs of American Colleges and Universities," *Modern Language Journal*, Vol. LII, No. 5 (May, 1968), pp. 470–480.
3. For example, the Department of Romance Languages at the University of Washington, Seattle, for practical pedagogical purposes, conducted testing in many beginning sections of French to compare AL-M trained students with those using *Parole et Pensée*. The results, which show higher scores for the latter, have not been published.
4. Kenneth D. Chastain & Frank J. Woerdehoff, "A Methodological Study Comparing the Audio-Lingual Habit Theory and the Cognitive Code-Learning Theory," *Modern Language Journal*, Vol. LII, No. 5 (May, 1968), pp. 268–279. This article notes a number of recent publications in which the validity of audio-lingual practices is questioned for lack of proof.
5. For example, The University of Washington, University of California, Berkeley, Stanford, and U.C.L.A.
6. See above, p. 86.
7. "The Colby College Conference on the Undergraduate Major in French," Jean D. Bundy *et al.*, *The French Review*, Vol. XLII, No. 1 (October, 1968), pp. 66–73.
8. *Ibid.*, p. 68.
9. *Slate Supplement to the General Catalogue*, Berkeley, A.S.U.C., Winter, 1967, p. 49.
10. *Ibid.*, Summer, 1967, p. 37.
11. *Ibid.*, Fall, 1967, p. 56.
12. *Academic Standing of Stanford Undergraduates*, Stanford, April, 1968.
13. Diane Pierson, Dominguez State College, Los Angeles, June, 1969.
14. Christian C. Finch, *Concours littéraire*, Stanford, 1969.
15. Bob Scott, *ibid.*, 1965.

4

Pierrette Spetz

THE VERBAL-ACTIVE METHOD
IN HIGH SCHOOL

IN attempting to define some of the problems of foreign language teaching on the high school level, one should first look carefully at present day high school students; they have changed considerably over the past decade. We could complain that they are more difficult to motivate, more easily bored, less polite, we could reasonably enough deplore their poor listening habits and the lamentable influence of the "third parent"—the television set in front of which they grew up—and we would not fail to mention their rebellious, or at least, disrespectful attitude toward authority. But, in a happier frame of mind, we might rejoice in their sincerity, in their acute critical thinking, in their demands for higher standards on our part, in their increasing dislike of wasted classroom time, and we might even welcome the daily challenge which they represent for us.

Most of them do not bother to dissimulate a yawn when they are bored, and they are also less apprehensive about showing their opposition to the rules, the system, the "establishment." They are quite often unwilling to make any effort unless they know why it is demanded of them. "Why do we have to study a foreign language?" "Why wear shoes?" "Why not slouch?" "Why did you make the past participle agree with the direct object?" "Why cut my hair?" "Why do you make us repeat it so many times?" Perhaps those questions would be terribly objectionable if we were trying to train the students like docile animals. But have we not hoped to develop more questioning minds and constructively critical human beings? Have we done the job too well?

Depending on our mood, age, degree of acceptance, ability to answer their questions and to help direct their efforts, we possibly view today's high school students as redoubtable monsters or as highly interesting individuals. In any case, we are witnessing changes that occur increasingly fast, and every change in the general atmosphere of the high school will continue to have its special effects on foreign language teaching.

Meanwhile, some of the seemingly timeless hurdles are still with us. Class size has remained a problem and has often become worse. In some cases it is assumed that the rate of attrition will be high—because "foreign languages are difficult"—therefore, large classes are formed. And when classes are large, there is less time for individual help and more students fail—a self-fulfilling prophecy. The language laboratory and modern methods have not performed the miracle which some expected. *Plus ça change plus c'est la même chose*, and the pupil-teacher ratio still matters, undoubtedly more than in most other disciplines.

Easy high school courses created to prevent the dropout have attracted many students away from the foreign language classroom, where hard work is often required, and where that work may not always appear especially meaningful. Only universities require a foreign language for admission, therefore many students naturally choose to postpone a difficult study.

The importance of grades in high school college preparatory classes cannot be minimized. Many students see no reason to continue in an exacting foreign language class when a vaguely cultural course will enable them to fulfill the grade requirements for the honor roll and for college admission. Moreover, foreign language teachers have almost traditionally been known as hard graders and not always objective graders. While many claim to give equal importance to oral and written work, very few let their actual grades reflect any such equality. Most teachers feel more sure of their written grades and of being able to justify them easily in case of conflict; they are also better trained to grade papers objectively than oral work.

In many classrooms mimic-memorization methods have at least achieved the goal of making every student "say something" in the foreign language. They have also simplified the work of some teachers, and they have enabled school districts to employ incompetent teachers who were simply expected to stay one dialogue ahead of the class. But problems of a more serious nature arose: "Kids in the lower grades may be willing to memorize dialogues and repeat phrases in a foreign tongue without really knowing what they mean. But as students get older, they run into a conflict. All their other school learning requires them to understand what they do and to ask questions when they didn't understand. In language classes, however, they must faithfully follow the lead of the teacher, must not speak or ask questions in English and must playact as if they were little children learning to speak for the first time. They constantly run the risk of making foolish mistakes in public. And the independent thinking, originality, and initiative encouraged in other classes are discouraged and even condemned in language classes."[1] An anti-intellectual theory of language learning could well convince the students that one can learn a language without thinking and that the goal is truly to become a linguistic robot: "Never mind what it means, just say it!" But such an order cannot be accepted by young people who have decided to re-examine everything, including their own language and their society's code of ethics! At a time when each student is bent upon "doing his thing," what could be less palatable than a ready-made dialogue that he not only has to memorize, but that he must also hear as many times as there are pairs of students in the class, much of the time not knowing too clearly what he is saying or hearing, and keenly aware of the uselessness of the whole process? Relevance is a word we often hear these days. Perhaps we should keep it in mind as we evaluate the materials and methods we use.

Most alert Americans realize with increasing clarity the need for foreign language learning and for effective communication with people of all nations. A large percentage of our students now travel abroad or otherwise come in contact with foreigners in their own country. We could, of course, consider at great length the role of foreign languages and literatures as humanistic studies, but such an undertaking would be beyond our purpose here. It is obvious that we cannot complacently let students turn away from foreign language studies. Methods will never render the study of a foreign language simple, but they can make it more meaningful, more effective, and more interesting. Boredom is surely the greatest enemy in any classroom, and our students are still quite willing to work hard, if the activities make sense to them, if they are challenging without being impossible. For those reasons, most of my observations will deal with a method which seems to be the most effective in the classroom because it provides active involvement for all students and encourages them to think in the foreign language. That is why Yvone Lenard described it several years ago as a verbal-active method, the basis of her *Parole et Pensée*.[2]

What Are Some of the Communication Patterns in the Foreign Language Classroom?

Each student becomes involved when he actively communicates in the foreign language, not when he simply repeats what someone else has devised. Communication should not just be an exchange of question-answers by the teacher and

 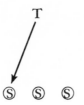 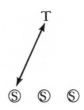

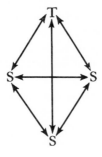

students; it really should include exchanges between students from the very beginning of the course. Naturally, this is very difficult to achieve with the standard seating arrangement, but one does not need to abide by that traditional plan even if the janitor does prefer it! A circle, or a U formation, or an occasional arrangement by small groups, is certainly more conducive to the teaching of conversation skills. Who wants to talk to someone's back? For many students, this is a very important—but also very threatening— activity: the first time they actually have to speak out in class. (We have some very quiet students who have sailed through eight or ten years of their education without making themselves heard in any language.) Although these are not the easiest to pronounce, a great and rather common way to start is to state, "*Je m'appelle. . . . Comment vous appelez-*

vous?" and have the students continue around the room as briskly as possible. Anyway, the class will function better if the students know one another. The same technique can be used for birthday, date of birth, family, pets, favorite subjects, etc., the students choosing the person whom they wish to address. There will be mistakes, corrections, repetitions, a loudness problem, but each student will learn to say correctly enough what he meant to say in the first place.

Even if they protest at first, students learn to accept and to enjoy a class which is different, a class in which no English is spoken. One way to set the tone is to take attendance by asking each student a brief question in French—not everyday, but often—and it does not take much time. As time goes by, we can ask more complex questions and tailor them to the individual: *"Comment va votre chien?"* or *"Allez-vous mieux?"* to the one who has been absent.

Should French Be the Exclusive Language of the Classroom?

There are varying points of view, but most teachers do agree that success depends a great deal upon the constant use of the target language. Using the foreign language all the time is possible and rewarding, although some teachers, especially in the beginning, may give certain clarifications in English while the students are only allowed to use the target language. Or, occasionally, but still exceptionally, questions in English may be asked during the last five minutes of the period if necessary. Certainly in the very early stages, the teacher should not feel guilty if he makes a brief remark in English necessitated by the conducting of classroom business, which may be a separate realm from the world of the foreign language. (Reading the school daily bulletin in any foreign language would be an awesome challenge for any teacher!) The pre-college teacher, particularly in the public schools, must find an intelligent compromise in making concessions to administrative and organizational needs. In the end, everyone feels greater satisfaction when using the target language exclusively.

Sometimes the teacher is more reluctant than the students to "play the game" consistently, partly because he may not be sure of the correct foreign words for common American expressions. How do you say "cheerleader" and "make-up test" in French? Also, conscientious educators want to be *sure* that they are clearly understood at all times, therefore, they use a great deal of English, speak about the foreign language, not in it, and promptly translate into English everything they have said in the foreign language. The students may not even try to understand the first utterance; they know it will be translated.

And then how does one explain a new vocabulary word without translating? Actually, that is rather easy with a little practice. At the elementary stages, the vocabulary is concrete, and we can often point to the objects, of course: *"C'est un porte-monnaie."* Then, we can follow, for example, de Sauzé's excellent model to teach the word *glace: "En été l'eau du lac est liquide; en hiver l'eau du lac n'est pas liquide, elle est solide, l'eau solide est de la glace."* For the student, this requires concentration, but it makes a more lasting impression besides giving him the joy of discovering a new word by his own effort. For the teacher, it is not the easiest way to communicate; he has to select known words or cognates, otherwise, his explanation will not be easily grasped.

Using a limited and carefully controlled vocabulary, a teacher can soon teach the entire lesson in the target language. In French, Spanish, and Italian, it is particularly easy to include the teaching of grammar in that statement, since the grammatical terms are so similar to the English ones. If a student understands plural, he also understands *pluriel* and *plurale*, the concepts may be difficult, the terms are not.

It is really amazing how few phrases the students need to know in the foreign language in order to ask all their questions and make all their remarks in that language: *"Que signifie... ?" "Comment dit-on... ?" "Je ne comprends pas..." "Ou est... ?" "Pourquoi... ?" "Il manque... "* constitute a fairly good start.

The fifty minute per day foreign language class will never be a substitute for the complete immersion which occurs when a person actually lives in the foreign country, but it is quite possible to create a suitable climate so that the student thinks in the foreign tongue during the greater part of the period. As Manual Salas says, "I am convinced that our fundamental premise must be recognition of the fact that we should teach contemporary foreign languages directly, in the languages themselves . . . English, then, should be banished from the classroom as radically as possible . . . Students should learn that meaning in the foreign language is often supremely independent from meaning in their mother tongue. The teacher and the foreign language atmosphere which he builds in his class should help the pupils to free their consciousness from the domination of English."[3]

What Will Our Students Memorize?

"We are training civilized and cultivated young people, not parrots that can only repeat phrases learned by rote or banalities fabricated in assembly line fashion . . ."[4]

Many foreign language teachers are now re-examining the dialogue-memorization method and discovering that its advantages are, to say the least, limited. In order to build up a stock from which one could pull out the right phrase at the right moment, one would have to memorize millions of utterances, a monumental task.

During the summer of 1967, a very important sports event brought together in the lobby of a small Amsterdam hotel the Olympic bicycle team of Mexico and a number of tourists. Everyone was eager to communicate, particularly a young American girl who confided to me, "They're so nice, I wish they had memorized 'my' dialogues! "

We do not mean to advocate the complete elimination of memorization; what teacher does not derive a great deal of satisfaction out of sending the students away in June with a few beautiful lines of poetry added to their cultural background? And some poems actually constitute aesthetic exercises in pronunciation and enunciation,[5] but most of the dialogues which have been written to date for language textbooks are not worth memorizing for any occasion and are hardly a substitute for Victor Hugo or Apollinaire.

Surely, learning the dictionary, as Gouin discovered, would never lead to the mastery of a language, and lists of disconnected words would not be helpful either toward the mastery of a language—if we consider mastery the ability to express one's own thoughts.

But we need to make students familiar enough with certain automatic responses so that they will reply rapidly and correctly. As explained by Yvone Lenard, most of those automatic responses are verb-centered, with special stress on the *je* and *vous* forms. For instance, the question "*Avez-vous... ?*" should bring "*Oui, j'ai...*" or "*Non, je n'ai pas...*" which are later modified into "*Je l'ai...*" "*Je les ai... *" "*J'en ai... *" "*J'en ai trop...*" etc. The question "*Y a-t-il... ?*" should elicit "*Il y a... *" "*Il n'y a pas de... *" then "*Il y en a... *" "*Il n'y en a pas...*" and "*Il n'y en a plus... *" Those are key patterns which lend themselves to an infinite variety of sentences and to the expression of many thoughts.

At all times, it is important for the students to know what they are "really" saying even in the most common phrases and idioms. They should know, for example, that the verb *voir* is in *voilà*, and that *pain* does not mean "gold" even if the French say "*bon comme le pain*" to signify "as good as gold." From the very beginning they must know that a foreign language is not simply a new set of words but a different point of view. Thus they will be prepared for *Vous me manquez, il me plait* and *ça ne se dit pas.* When he was comparing his two autobiographies, the bilingual author Julian Green aptly remarked, "I did not say in English what I would have said in French. Speaking a language means adopting a way of life."

We need to ask of our students much more than the memorization of phrases or patterns. We can propose a fresh outlook on the world and even encourage the acceptance of a different way of thinking. "And how much is it in *real* money?" asked the American tourist in a Mexican shop. The discipline to which I am referring would be valuable not only in the students' academic progress but also in developing an attitude of tolerance which is at least as important.

What About Grammar?

When the grammar-translation method was labelled traditional, old fashioned, and obsolete, both of the words, grammar and translation, took on a negative connotation and many teachers accepted the concept that "language is something you do." Therefore, they attempted to develop solely automatic responses and asked the students not to analyze what they were saying.

But some students never gave up. They kept wanting to know why we say *le, la, les,* when and why. And that is grammar. Languages are living, reasonable, and, in spite of their oddities, logical. Grammar is a convenient set of rules which enables the student, as Piaget says, to "reinvent" the language in his own mind. It also enables the teacher to capitalize upon the fact that he is teaching intelligent people with a certain level of maturity. For the same reason, etymology, the study of word derivation, of roots, prefixes and suffixes can be useful if the students become capable of making educated guesses and exciting discoveries about the meaning of new words. It would be impossible and not advisable to spend a great deal of class time on that study in the high school, but students can be encouraged to look for clues and links which make learning more logical and more durable.

We live in a system-oriented society where even the most humble worker needs to have a modicum of understanding of the system in which he is involved. Many people like to seek and discover some order in life, in their surroundings and in their language. It confers greater predictability to future events and a greater feeling of security. Even children seem to have instinctive, built-in grammar and it may lead them astray—"You *teached* it to us yesterday."—but it certainly makes sense.

Teaching the grammar of any language for grammar's sake is, hopefully, a thing of the past. There seems to be little value in memorizing rules verbatim, and the modern emphasis is better placed on the application of the rules: nobody wants to eat the recipe, everybody prefers the cake! And let's admit it, the main reason some of us know the rules of agreement of the past participles so well is that copying those rules a number of times was used as a punishment for almost any offense by unimaginative French teachers.

Actually, anyone can memorize the rule of agreement of the past participles, or any other rule. But having memorized it does not necessarily enable one to use it correctly, particularly if one is not quite sure of the meaning of key terms such as "direct object" or "precede." A less learned, but very effective rule, for example, was given by Mary P. Conrad some years ago: "The past participle, being a verbal adjective, agrees in number and gender with whichever definite, preceding word it *logically* modifies. This includes all the other rules."[6] For many students, we have found it easier yet to ask that they write like a mediocre secretary who does not go back on what she has written. For instance: *J'ai admiré les tableaux*. When she writes *admiré*, she does not know what has been admired, therefore, she can't make it agree. But in the sentence beginning with *Les tableaux que j'ai admirés...* she knows that the paintings were the admired objects and she writes *admirés* with *s*. The same is true with the auxiliary verb *être*. When she writes *tombée* in the sentence *La petite fille est tombée* she knows exactly who fell and makes the past participle agree with *petite fille*. There are many approaches, but the one which works is the correct one for each student and, in some cases, there are students who don't even seem to need the rule! It is clear that *reasoning* about the nature of thinking in a language facilitates the assimilation of what is already logical.

Another example we would like to mention deals with the change of accent in certain French verbs. Some students have such a good ear that they automatically write forms such as *Je répète* with the correct accent marks, with no hesitation at all. Others need to know that there is a grave accent because the word ends with a mute "e" preceded by a consonant. Some learn to perform the same operation by analogy with a simple word like *père*. Others still learn the whole present tense with a shoe-shaped diagram:

Je répète	Nous répétons
Tu répètes	Vous répétez
Il répète	Ils répètent

Most students do not have extensive familiarity with the grammar of their own language, and we cannot expect the entire English curriculum to be revised to serve our purpose. Some teachers feel that it helps to teach a lesson in English grammar first and separately if they want to be absolutely sure that the students understand clearly such concepts as infinitive, adverb, direct object, adjective, etc. If that is done, such a lesson should be very brief, practical, and to the point, and should be aimed at establishing a simple analogy or contrast with the foreign language.

In teaching the grammar of the foreign language, one should also keep technical explanations to a minimum, going from the example to the rule and from the rule to immediate, extensive practice. For instance, all books being closed, the teacher says very clearly: *"Y a-t-il des fleurs dans la salle de classe?"* *"Non, il n'y a pas de fleurs."* Other examples are given with student participation until someone asks: *"Pourquoi dites-vous 'de'?"* and the teacher explains: *"Parce que la phrase est négative. On dit 'de' à la place de 'un,' 'une,' 'des,' 'du,' etc. dans une phrase négative, sauf après le verbe être."* Then the students are ready to practice sentences with *de* and others in which it is precluded by the use of *être*.

Many active "tricks" can be used to enliven the teaching of grammar and to reinforce what has been taught. For instance, the teacher can start a drawing on the blackboard—a roof—saying: *"Sur ma maison, il y a un toit."* He passes the chalk to a student who adds another part of the house and makes a similar statement, for instance, *"Il y a une antenne de télévision."* When the drawing looks complete enough, the teacher starts erasing one feature after the other and the class, or one student at a time, declares: *"Il n'y a pas de cheminée."* *"Il n'y a pas de porte."* etc. Thus, we have reinforced the lesson on *de* in a negative sentence and reviewed some useful vocabulary.

Whether one uses the inductive or deductive approach to the teaching of grammar, the emphasis should be on the application and not on the verbalization of the rule. Most of all, it must be remembered that grammar is the system which enables the student to combine words in an infinity of sentences to express his own thoughts. We must make no apology for teaching it, and we need not call it by some other name like "generalizations" or "tips." Grammar has its own rightful place in the foreign language classroom, in spite of those who are indifferent to making our students illiterate in two languages.

What Is Meant by Single Emphasis?

At the high school level, it is particularly important and particularly difficult to avoid confusing the students. We can only teach *one* point at a time, not too slowly or they would become bored, but not too fast, because it is naturally easier to make a point clear when it is new than when they have already made mistakes and practiced, by repetition, the wrong way.

De Sauzé recommends, for instance, that only one gender be introduced at first in elementary German, and of course, only in the nominative case. In French, although it seems logical to teach *y* and *en* together, high school students seem to fare better if thoroughly drilled on the meaning and uses of *en* before going on to the other adverbial pronoun.

Many teachers have also found that students learn all the verb tenses better if they are only faced with the present tense during the first year, and if each conjugation is introduced after the previous one has been well assimilated. That is what de Sauzé calls "the incubation period," or, as the French say, *le temps détruit ce que l'on fait sans lui*.

Probably the greatest mistakes made by beginning teachers are caused by an enthusiastic desire to teach too much too fast. The same fault can be found in many of the so-called audio-lingual methods: "The average dialogue in use today presents anywhere from eight to twenty different utterances which represent many linguistic problems. It is not uncommon to find as many as ten or eleven different sentence patterns in a single dialogue, not to mention the problems of linking, liaison, and elision that may occur within these types, and it is rare to find more than two or three treated in the pattern drills that follow . . . such procedures do the student more harm than good. He does learn to produce a given number of utterances in each unit, but these are meaningful to him only in terms of English and only in the exact form found in the unit."[7]

Single emphasis and spacing the difficulties over a period of time are only two of the common sense rules of foreign language teaching of which we sometimes need to be reminded. A third, which we are sometimes forced to break, is the one which recommends proceeding from the simple to the complex. That is because natives have an instinctive way of using the most complex forms of their language to say the simplest things. A two-year-old bambino can say *"Vorrei avere molto denaro."* without knowing that he is using a conditional; French children can say *"j'y vais"* at an early age, and it does not seem to trouble them that the most commonly used verbs are irregular.

What should a foreign language teacher do? Shall we substitute nice regular but seldom used verbs for the ones the natives use and follow the old textbooks which had *Je désire une pomme* because *désirer* is regular and *vouloir* is not? Obviously, we have to teach some common irregular verbs at a very early stage. We find ourselves only too easily in situations where we are compelled to teach *je voudrais, s'il vous plaît* and *je m'appelle* long before the students can know everything about those constructions. Using less-used cognates *(désirer* for *vouloir, similaire* for *pareil,* etc.) is merely a provisional concession whose place should be largely reserved for material intended for listening-comprehension or introducing the meaning of the non-cognate form. One should not allow the learner to acquire actively the uncommon alternate. Fortunately, with few exceptions, we should and can proceed step by step, from the simple to the complex, in an orderly manner, always integrating the new material with that which has already been assimilated.

Why Do We Need a Multiple Approach?

Few subjects demand as much of a high school student as the foreign language class. He must be a good listener, he must be flexible and versatile enough to change his speech patterns and to make the switch into a totally new means of expression. He must adopt a new symbolic system at an age when he is still working on that of his own language, and he must learn to read in a different key with a new set of sounds. He needs all the assistance we can give him.

Our experience leads us to advocate the order hear/speak-write/read, but without specifying the most appropriate time to introduce students to the written language, because that time varies with the teachers' techniques and with the students' abilities. At the beginning of the audio-lingual revolution, many teachers thought that pronunciation and aural comprehension would be greatly facilitated by delaying exposure to the written language for weeks or even months, and that may have proven true with younger children. But on the high school level, while it seems advantageous to present all new material orally first, there seems to be little gain in delaying the introduction of writing because our students will attempt to take notes anyway, and since they are already familiar with a symbolic system, they are conditioned to expect another.

Hearing, speaking, writing, and reading reinforce each other and play a different role with different students simply because people learn differently. Some students never really learn a new word until they have written it repeatedly in a context, others learn better through their ears, but they all need a certain amount of all types of practice. As nearly every public high school teacher knows, we generally cannot allow students to take such dangerous weapons as pens and pencils to the language laboratory. And that unfortunately precludes laboratory workbooks or worksheets. But we can assign—as written homework—the very exercises which are done in the lab whenever they lend themselves to such practice. What we find objectionable about methods favoring grammar or dialogues or reading to the point of excluding almost completely the other approaches is that they do not take into account individual differences and the fact that each skill helps reinforce the others.

Did Theseus really kill Procrustes, the robber who stretched or amputated the limbs of travelers to make them conform to the length of his bed, or has the famous monster found refuge in some foreign language classrooms?

What About the Language Laboratory?

In 1958, a foreign language teacher could still get some applause when she concluded her speech with: "And remember, fellow teachers, that we all learned French *without a language laboratory.*" And she was right; many of her listeners had acquired their fluency by living in France and attending French universities, a much more natural way than the language laboratory, but not within everyone's reach. Besides, hardly everyone has the linguistic aptitude that most foreign language teachers have.

As foreign language teachers, we should recall the story of Aesop whom his master Xanthos had sent to the market for the purpose of buying the very best he could find. Aesop brought back nothing but tongue, assuming that nothing could be better than the tongue which is used for social life, reasoning, the search for truth and prayer. But when the next day, his master ordered him to purchase the very worst thing he could find, Aesop again brought back nothing but tongue because nothing could be worse than the tongue which is at the origin of arguments, dissension, war, error, slander and blasphemy. That story could be interpreted in a number of ways, but it seems most appropriate with regard to the language laboratory. The years between 1960 and 1970 have seen its rise in importance, but will the next decade see its fall? Such seems to be the case in some schools where the laboratory is used so little that plans are being made to reconvert it into a classroom.

When laboratories were first presented to teachers, they were labeled "the promised land." And, in many cases, the lab has done much to help students develop better accents, greater fluency, more self-confidence. It has provided them with individual monitoring, individual instruction in spite of the large classes. It has made the quiet students speak up in the privacy of the booth and perhaps also in class. Most of all, it has improved the students' ability to perceive differences in sounds and to reproduce them acceptably well.

The mechanical aspects frightened some teachers: what if something should go wrong? Often, something did, but major problems—those which make the laboratory unusable—were rare, and all went well, especially for the teachers fortunate enough to have one or two more booths than students. "Let's make friends with the beast," recommended laboratory advocates, and women teachers, who had never operated any device more complex than an electric sewing machine, found themselves adept enough to use the laboratory painlessly and successfully.

What really went wrong? While electronics companies kept improving the quality and performance of the equipment, the really good tapes were—and still are—rare. Any error on a tape can have serious consequences by its very role as a model. Some textbook publishers rushed into making tapes and produced obviously poor ones. Others, with the best intentions in the world, produced tapes of a quality acceptable to the teachers but deadly boring to the students. Television advertising has trained them (luckily?) to turn off what they do not find interesting and that is just what they did when they were asked to repeat dull sentences unrelated to their experiences.

Every laboratory exercise should be examined very critically: "Does anyone ever say that?" and if the honest answer is "Probably not," the exercise is not acceptable, for here we are dealing with active learning. Every utterance should have the quality of naturalness and spontaneity. Also, there should be very few plain repetition drills because they succeed only in putting the students to sleep. Instead, exercises should be varied and require that the students think.

The language laboratory, while it frees the student of the presence of his amused and critical peers, also involves a degree of loneliness. If the student is shy, he is content to remain quietly in his booth, and it may be a while before the teacher realizes that he is not performing. Certainly, students should never be brought to the language laboratory to repeat material they do not already know, but suppose they forget? How many will dare to raise their hand and ask for help? Because it is hard to see each student, teachers have to be even more alert in the laboratory than in the classroom. Some teachers use the blackboard of the laboratory; they write reminders (verb endings, pronoun chart) for those who learn more slowly. One can play an exercise once with the clues on the board, then erase the clues and replay the same exercise. This is particularly important when doing an exercise on minimal pairs for students who do not really hear the differences very well, e.g. *je l'ai* and *je l'aime*.

In public high schools, teachers have to accompany the students to the language laboratory in order to prevent naps and vandalism; therefore, laboratory time cuts into class time. How much time can we afford to spend in the lab? How can we retain the time needed to teach the other skills? Many teachers find that good results are obtained when the laboratory is used two or three times per week, for twenty minute sessions, with careful planning and flexibility. But if the tapes are good, the results justify the efforts. The laboratory can provide a variety of voices and accents, a valuable reinforcement of the lesson, and a great deal of individual instruction. The students also are exposed to a welcome change of scenery. Finally, the teacher's voice can rest from the twenty-five period per week strain.

It remains true that repetition without understanding is the most sinful waste of school time and that all practice should be audio-lingual-*mental*. The quality of the material used in the lab makes an infinite difference, and even the best materials should be re-examined and brought up to date frequently so that they will continue to reflect a living language.

The recent (1969) Pennsylvania study "challenges the effectiveness of both the audio-lingual approach and the language laboratory" by showing that "the use of the lab had no discernible effects in either speaking or listening."[8] While that study seems disturbing to some, it may also point to the need for better materials and higher standards of teaching in the language laboratory. In this profession, we must re-evaluate constantly what we are doing. We can never sit back, relax and let the hardware take over. We *are* needed.

Starting to Write in the Foreign Language

Small, unsung miracles occur everyday in the foreign language classroom: there is the day a shy student is *really* heard speaking a whole sentence in the target language, the day when oral compositions are first presented, the day when we tell a joke in the foreign language and they all laugh. But one of the most important steps is taken when our students begin to associate the sound and the orthography of the language, when our students write. And their progress in the written language almost always closely parallels their progress in the spoken language.

"You know," said a French IV girl, "I really believe that during the past four years I have written more French for this class than English for my English class!"

Most of the writing of a high school foreign language student is done at home, at least during the first two years. Later, it resembles the work done in the mother tongue: essays, note taking, dissertations, *explications de texte*, book reports.

One of the first written exercises which we do in the foreign language classroom is the dictation: number dictation, then dictation of short phrases followed by sentences and by short narratives. In the classrooms of France, the dictation has long been a ritual. A rather difficult passage of literature is selected by the teacher and dictated to the nervous students, who live in awe of the five-mistake limit. It is often full of difficult agreements and *pluriels douteux* and constitutes a serious hurdle in the way of a student's promotion to the next grade level.

In the foreign language classroom, even if it is used as a test, the dictation is usually much less frightening because it is based on known material. Mistakes may be due to lack of vocabulary, poor auditory comprehension, poor concentration, or grammatical problems. For instance, if we dictate: *"Il commence à parler."* we may assume that the students who wrote: *"Il comment sapparlay."* had a rather serious comprehension problem, whereas the one who wrote: *"Il commence à parlé"* may simply need to be reminded of the use of an infinitive after a conjugated verb.

If vandalism does not seem to be a problem, we can give the dictation in the language laboratory, but even if that is not possible, many teachers like to give taped dictation. It is a better attention developing device, because the students know that they cannot stop the tape, slow it down or look at it with beseeching eyes. It may also have the definite advantage of bringing into the classroom a different voice and perhaps a different accent.

We recommend using a good, but fairly short *dictée* at the end of a unit, as a review device. It can be done in this fashion: a volunteer goes to the rear blackboard and writes the dictation while the rest of the class writes on paper without looking at the blackboard. The teacher proceeds in the usual manner: reads the text, dictates with punctuation, reads again.

When that has been done, the students proofread their paper before turning around to look at the blackboard. Then a student is asked to read and criticize the first sentence, corrections are made, questions are answered, and the students make a note of the mistakes they have made in order to review those points of grammar and vocabulary with special attention. We continue in this way until the whole dictation has been corrected.

In French I, an eight or ten sentence dictation is sufficient and will require about twenty minutes of class time, because questions often arise in the course of the correction. We have to keep each activity fairly short and probably cannot give more than one dictation per week or every other week. If we spend ten minutes correcting the homework, twenty minutes on a dictation, and five minutes making an assignment for the next day, we have only a quarter of an hour for oral activities, for introducing a new item or for a laboratory session, assuming that all goes well, that there is no fire drill, no announcement on the public address system, no early dismissal due to a ballgame or field trip. And there *are* days when all goes well.

What About Homework?

What kind of homework should we give during the first two years? The worst kind would probably be the translation type which used to be the most common. It is rather easy to give assignments which are solely in the target language: a set of oral or written questions on the reading selection, a short oral or written composition, some blanks to fill with the vocabulary or verb forms which are being studied, with a recommendation to fill them in *"d'une manière intelligente,"* a set of questions to answer, answers for which the students have to write the corresponding questions, and many others.

One of the best reasons for giving a short homework assignment is that we can require higher standards of performance ("You mean that we have to think?") and even capitalization and punctuation. Another reason is that the assignment is meaningless unless we correct it, and correcting it takes time. In the foreign language classroom, all new material has to be introduced, thoroughly explained, and practiced in class, as well as be integrated with what has preceded. Therefore, we have to arrange our time carefully, still providing some leeway to answer questions thoroughly and courteously.

When the written homework requires rather standard answers, we can call as many students' names as there are items and have the students write them on the board. Twenty or twenty-five students may be out of their seats at the same time and there may be some busy noise for a very short time. Students frequently help one another even if they have not been assigned to work as a team, but that collaboration is usually beneficial. Then, each student reads "his" sentence to the class and students point to the errors which are promptly corrected. This goes rather fast, and it can be speeded up if we call the students to the blackboard as we take attendance, being careful not to select consistently the students at the head of the list. While the homework is being corrected, class members should feel free to ask questions and to provide opportunities for the teacher to clarify the difficult points.

If the homework exercise consisted of filling blanks, we can call on students at random, asking them to read the entire sentence and to spell out the word which they had to provide. They should be able to spell aloud clearly and with confidence in the target language.

If the homework consisted of a composition or of some original answers which will vary from one student to the next, it is more advisable to collect it and to grade it. If time is short, we do not need to correct the errors, we can simply underline the errors and ask the student to correct them for the next day with or without our help. They can usually correct most of their mistakes, which are often errors due to carelessness.

Few textbooks provide enough exercises, and foreign language teachers are kept busy making worksheets. One of the most unattractive features of the homework we generally give is its fragmentary aspect. We go from *De quelle couleur est votre auto?* to *Où est l'Arc de Triomphe?* Some *"coq-à-l'âne"* types of exercise may be inevitable, but one could never encourage enough the use of the short composition as early as possible in order to train the students to express their own ideas in the foreign language. "But do they possess enough vocabulary for originality?" "Can they manipulate with any variety the simple structures they know?" We do not really always know. Some French I students may surprise us, but, if we refuse them the opportunity, they never will!

Whatever the assignment, it should have a problem-solving attractiveness, so that the students will find some degree of satisfaction in doing it. Most of all, students should never have to copy the book, and they should not have to study on their own new material which has not yet been explained. If the home assignments are a valid extension of the classroom work, students who do them well and regularly should progress much better than their less studious classmates, and they should be aware of that advantage. Doing the homework simply because the teacher said so is fast becoming an obsolete practice.

"If the homework is oral, they don't do it," complain some teachers. Actually, that may be true of a memorized dialogue, but it's rarely true of an oral composition. At first, the topics are rather simple and concrete, but they do not need to be childish: my house, my family, my friend, a favorite class, a favorite person. The way the students treat them is often quite interesting, and the quality improves steadily. Until the students develop a certain feeling for it, it is best to limit the time. They can say a great deal in one or two minutes if they have planned their talk. Two of the main problems are time and boredom. In a class of forty students, it would take 120 minutes with no interruptions to hear three-minute talks. But with the inevitable breaks, we would need three complete class periods. We simply could not do it. Many teachers find it best not to have more than ten oral compositions any day, and, if a class is large, we are forced to reduce even more that valuable activity.

In second-year classes and in the subsequent courses, the variety of topics is endless, and boredom is practically eliminated, especially if the students are allowed to select their own topics. For instance: *Faut-il apprendre le latin?, Peut-on vivre sans télévision?, Combien de fois par semaine faut-il prendre un bain?*, and when the students have their choice of topic with only the restriction that they must use the conditionnel: *Si le monde était carré... , Si j'étais un garçon... , Si les professeurs s'arrêtaient de donner des devoirs... , Si on abolissait l'éducation physique... , Si on abolissait la police... .*

In the preparation of both oral and written compositions, students frequently face a problem of vocabulary and conscientiously try to use a dictionary. While a dictionary is a valuable device for the advanced student, it may become an obstacle to learning in the hands of a beginner. For one thing, what good is it if the student uses a term (in an oral presentation) that only he and the teacher understand? Furthermore, the dangers of misuse are serious: *"La petite fille 'larme' sa robe."* (tear) or *"On jouait les grands 'organes' de l'église pour le mariage."*

The advanced student can check the meaning of a new word in an all-French dictionary; he can give a definition of it to the class in the target language, and he can actually impart to his fellow students his newly acquired knowledge. By the third or fourth year, he is wary of idiomatic expressions such as "to run for office." He has learned to think critically and creatively in the foreign language. He is on his way to bilingualism. At that point, he can be trusted with a dictionary.

Reading Selections

The reading selection should be helpful in creating interest and in making the idioms and vocabulary more easily retainable. Students may not remember that we are on lesson seventeen but they all know that we are on the beach, *sur la plage*. People could undoubtedly learn a foreign language without a single *lecture*, but the narrative provides an interesting unity, it shows how the language works. It is particularly effective if it relates to the students' interests: sports, school, cars, dates, movies, television, all topics dear to high school students. On the other hand, we "lose" a class more easily with a childish narrative than with one which is a little above their level of maturity.

We introduce the narrative orally, books closed, our goal being to bridge the gap between what is known and what is new. Let us assume, for instance, that we are introducing Mrs. Lenard's story on the beach,[9] which will have as its grammatical focus the inchoative verbs. We can start by asking any student to show the map of France: *"Où est la carte?"* —they have known that for a long time. Now, someone shows the Mediterranean, the *Côte d'Azur*. We make them say all they know about the sea, the boats, the coast. The teacher or a student draws a coastline on the blackboard, we add waves, boats, sand, talking about each item and reviewing: *Il y a du sable... sur le sable, il y a... il n'y a pas de...* Once we have set the stage and involved as many students as possible in doing so, the new vocabulary is easy to teach. The word *maillot* is hard to pronounce, so we ask many questions: *De quelle couleur est votre maillot? Avez-vous un maillot neuf cette année? Où préférez-vous acheter un maillot?* Sea shells, sand castles appear.... If someone still does not understand *sable*, it is easy to draw an hourglass on the blackboard. Should we teach the same lesson a hundred times, there would always be new questions, new ways to explain the vocabulary!

Now, having everyone's attention, we are ready to look at

our arm and to state theatrically: *A la plage, moi, je rougis,* (or *je brunis,* or *je ne brunis pas...*), then involving each student in the exchange of views and problems: *Vous êtes blonde, est-ce que vous brunissez?* or *Suzie, demandez à Pierre s'il brunit ou s'il rougit au soleil,* and so on; the idea is to link clearly *brun-brunir, rouge-rougir, blanc-blanchir.*

When the material is understood, it is time to read the story to the class or to let the tape do it for us with expression and a variety of voices. The advantages of proceeding that way are obvious; if we had just opened the books and let the class take turns reading, we would have had some terribly mispronounced words and the students would not understand what they were reading.

There is not enough time for everyone to read the whole passage aloud, but the students should be prepared enough so that they can practice alone and be ready to answer questions on the narrative. We can assign a few questions as written or oral homework and ask the class to become familiar enough with the material to answer spontaneously any question on a similar topic. It is always beneficial to make students ask questions as well as answer them. To make sure that they speak loud enough and that the whole class is listening, it is best to select students who sit at a certain distance from each other.

The narrative is not to be memorized, of course, it is mostly used to provide a pertinent subject as a starting point for discussion and practice. A relevant reading presented in a lively way can indeed be very stimulating. And the questions (those from the book and many more) constitute an excellent means of checking on comprehension and of improving oral fluency without recourse to translation.

The Importance of Aural Comprehension

While we remain in the target language at all times, most students become accustomed to deriving meaning directly from the spoken language with its special hurdles of *liaisons* and *élisions* as well as from the written word. But it is nevertheless important, once in a while, to give an exercise or a test on just that one phrase of foreign language work; *aural comprehension*, particularly when good taped exercises exist with a variety of voices.

The students hear a short but meaningful conversation spoken at normal speed, preferably in the language laboratory. Then, they are given a dittoed set of questions (five or six) which they take a few minutes to examine. They may ask to have any word of the questions explained to them in the target language, or any new word that was on the tape. The tape is played once or twice more. If we do not allow any writing in the foreign language laboratory, we take the class back to the classroom where they answer the questions immediately.

As to grading this type of work, it is well to remember that it is an oral activity, resembling in a way what might occur if the students were in a foreign country. We therefore place little emphasis on the spelling and grammatical accuracy of the answers, grading solely or mostly on comprehension. The point in question remains whether the student understood or not, as it is in a real conversation.

Grading

If our policy or our department's policy is to give equal weight to oral and written grades, an easy way to insure that we carry out the policy is to keep those scores separately (two separate pages, two different colors)—oral grades for aural comprehension exercises, oral compositions, and tests; written scores for homework, tests, and quizzes. Using the point system, let's assume that we do not come out even and that we end the quarter with a larger number of possible points on the written side, for instance. It is easy to reestablish the balance by using a coefficient to equalize the total number of points attainable in both oral and written work. (If seventy-five points were possible on the written work but only fifty on the oral work, we simply multiply all written scores by the fraction two-thirds or all oral scores by three-halves.)

Naturally, the students should know how they are graded and we can give them a form on which they keep a record of their own points. Such a practice tends to minimize conflicts at the end of the quarter and students realize that the responsibility for improving their scores rests with them and not the teacher's whims.

Keeping score and giving grades which are as objective as they can be do not exempt teachers from another type of evaluation. For instance, it is not uncommon for a high school student who sees "90%" on his test paper to ask, "Is that good?" or "Am I doing better?" which leads us to the important problem of individual—or person to person—evaluation. Many very good students need constant reassurance although their progress seems obvious to their teachers, parents, and classmates. A very good paper should always be returned with a complimentary word in the target language even if that means writing *Très bien* on the same student's papers week after week to acknowledge his perseverance. And a well-deserved *C'est bien* tends to incite any student to additional efforts. The same applies to oral work and to monitoring in the foreign language laboratory. If it is well to correct faulty pronunciation, it is just as essential to say *Bravo*, or some more moderate type of compliment, gauging our applause according to the effort and to the student's personality. Each student learns in a different way and also reacts to praise and criticism in a different way. If, as we previously said, boredom is probably the greatest enemy of the foreign language teacher, discouragement is next in line, and a student should never leave our class under an impression of failure and despair.

Our Role as Teachers

What students learn in the foreign language classroom is not only a new language and a new way of thinking. It is also a method of work and a greater appreciation of effort and accuracy. And since we all learn more by example than any other way, let us not forget that standards apply to us first of all. We mean, of course, all standards of good teaching in general, plus some which apply more specifically in foreign language teaching.

Even as we teach a beginners' class, we keep in mind that the students might possibly continue to study the language. Why teach *Pourquoi est-ce que vous écrivez?* exclusively when we know that they will, later, be instructed to use the inversion after interrogative adverbs? We have to teach the basic language while preparing for future developments and not simply to enable our students to "get along" in a foreign hotel or restaurant.

It takes both planning and integrity to avoid statements which are simple, convenient, and general, but not entirely true, such as: "Never use a conditional or a future after '*si*.'" (What about, *Je ne sais pas si je partirai en vacances?*) or "Never say '*de le*,' say '*du*,' forgetting about, "*J'ai oublié de le faire*." and all other uses of *le, la, les* as pronouns. Oversimplification might lead us to ridiculous situations almost comparable to that of the three great language professors in *Gulliver's Travels:* "The first object was to shorten discourse, by cutting polysyllables into one, and leaving out verbs and participles; because in reality all things imaginable are but nouns. The other project was a scheme for entirely abolishing all words whatsoever . . ."

Teaching beginners in any discipline always represents an enormous responsibility. While a large number of our students may not go beyond the requirements for entering a university, some of the more interested and more capable ones will undoubtedly go on to more advanced studies. In the same way as some of us were truly inspired to teach foreign languages by one or two outstanding teachers, students might be sufficiently motivated by *our* classes to come and join our ranks; we are teaching our future colleagues. That alone is reason enough to do the job exceedingly well!

Furthermore, while we are demanding a great deal of involvement and participation from our students, we need to remember how it feels to learn a foreign language—perhaps by learning a new one ourselves every ten years. We should be reminded that many of our students will not major in our field and that a mistake, however serious it might seem, is not a sin. We foreign language Teachers who teach our native tongue probably need the reminder more than anyone else, plus an extra dose of tolerance. *Celui qui pourrait tout comprendre voudrait tout pardonner.*

While we have examined here some of the current problems of high school foreign language teaching and some ways in which we have attempted to solve them with the verbal-active method, the list of both problems and solutions should end with *etc.* New problems arise everyday as a result of new laws and new attitudes among students and adults. There is little evidence that foreign language teaching will become any easier with time. While testing and exploiting every worthwhile new device and technique, we should neither overrate the magic methods nor underestimate our greatest allies: the students' interest, curiosity, and reasoning power.

Notes

1. Harry Reinert, *Bulletin of the National Association of Secondary School Principals*, Washington, 1966.

2. "It is a very active method, in which the student is constantly called on to perform in all the aspects of a language, to use his creativity within the framework of the structures learned, and in which the verb is considered the core of the sentence." Yvone Lenard, *Parole et Pensée du Professeur*, New York, Harper & Row, 1965, p. 4.

3. Manual Salas, Paper read to the Foreign Language Teachers Association of the State of Arizona, November 1959.

4. Roger Asselineau, "Language and Literature," *The French Review*, Vol. XXXVII, No. 6, May 1964, p. 684. (This particular issue is extremely relevant to the problems we are discussing here.)

5. "*Chat, chat, chat, charmant chat couché...*"

6. Mary P. Conrad, "A simple, Logical Rule for the Agreement of the Past Participle," *The French Review*, Vol. XXXVII, No. 4, February 1964, pp. 450–452.

7. Leo. L. Kelly, "Dialogue vs Structure," *The French Review*, Vol. XXXVII, No. 4, February 1964, pp. 432–439.

8. Philip Smith, "Static in the Language Lab." *Today's Education*, Vol. 58, No. 7, October 1969.

9. Yvone Lenard, *Parole et Pensée*, pp. 189–191.

REFERENCES

Asselineau, Roger, "Language and Literature," *The French Review*, Vol. XXXVII, No. 6 (May, 1964), p. 684.

Berko, Jean, "The child's learning of English morphology," *Word* 14, 1958, pp. 150–177.

Black, Max, *Models and Metaphors: Studies in Language and Philosophy*. Ithaca: Cornell University Press, 1962.

Bloomfield, Leonard, *An Introduction to the Study of Language*. New York: Henry Holt and Co., 1914.

——————, *Language*. New York: Holt, Rinehart, and Winston, 1933.

——————, *Outline Guide for the Practice Study of Foreign Languages*. Baltimore: Linguistic Society of America, 1942.

Brooks, Nelson, "Language Learning: The New Approach," *Phi Delta Kappan*, Vol. XLVII, No. 7, 1966.

Bundy, Jean D. *et al*, "The Colby Conference on the Undergraduate Major in French," *French Review*, Vol. XLII, No. 1 (October, 1968), pp. 66–73.

Carroll, John B., *The Foreign Language Attainments of Language Majors in the Senior Year*. Cambridge, Mass.: Harvard University, 1967.

Chastain, Kenneth D., and Woerdehoff, Frank J., "A Methodological Study Comparing the Audio-Lingual Habit Theory and the Cognitive Code-Learning Theory,"

Modern Language Journal, Vol. LII, No. 5 (May, 1968), pp. 268–279.

Chomsky, Noam, *Aspects of the Theory of Syntax*. Cambridge: M. I. T. Press, 1965.

————————, *Cartesian Linguistics*. New York: Harper & Row, 1966.

————————, "Linguistic Theory," *Reports of the Working Committees, Northeast Conference on the Teaching of Foreign Languages*. New York: MLA Materials Center, 1966.

————————, *Language and Mind*, New York: Harcourt, Brace, & World, 1968.

Concours littéraire. Stanford: Department of French and Italian, 1965, 1969.

Conrad, Mary P., "A Simple, Logical Rule for the Agreement of the Past Participle," *The French Review*, Vol. XXXVII, No. 4 (February, 1964), pp. 450–452.

Dacanay, Fe R., *Techniques and Procedures in Second Language Teaching*. Quezon City: Phoenix Publishing House, 1963.

de Sauzé, Emile B., *The Cleveland Plan for the Teaching of Modern Languages*. Philadelphia: John C. Winston Co., 1929; rev. ed. 1953.

Diller, Karl C., *Two Theories of Language as Approaches to Foreign Language Teaching*. Cambridge: Unpublished Ph.D. thesis, Harvard University Department of Linguistics, 1967. Forthcoming in book form as *Linguistic Theories and Foreign Language Teaching*.

Fodor, Jerry A., and Jerrold J. Katz, *The Structure of Language*. Englewood Cliffs: Prentice-Hall, 1964.

Gouin, François, *L'Art d'enseigner et d'étudier les langues*. Paris: Fischbacher, 1880. Translated by Howard Swan and Victor Bétis as *The Art of Teaching and Studying Languages*. London: George Philip and Son, Ltd., 1892.

Gut, Ann, "Programs of American Colleges and Universities," *Modern Language Journal*, Vol. LII, No. 5 (May, 1968), pp. 470–480.

Halle, Morris, "Phonology in Generative Grammar," *Word* 18, 1962, pp. 54–72. Reprinted in Fodor and Katz, 1964.

——————, "On the Bases of Phonology," in Fodor and Katz, 1964.

Haugen, Einar, "Linguists and the Wartime Program of Language Teaching," *Modern Language Journal* Vol. XXXIX, 1955, pp. 243–245.

——————, "Bilingualism as a Goal in Foreign Language Teaching," *On Teaching English to Speakers of Other Languages, Series One: Papers read at the TESOL conference, Tucson, Arizona, May, 1964.* Champaign: National Council of Teachers of English, 1965.

Heness, Gottlieb, *Der Leitfaden für den Unterricht in der Deütschen Sprache, ohne Sprachlehre und Wörterbuch,* 2nd Edition, with an introduction in English. Boston: Schönhof und Möller, 1875.

Hill, Archibald A., "Grammaticality," *Word* 17, 1961, pp. 1–10.

Hockett, Charles F., *A Course in Modern Linguistics.* New York: The Macmillan Co., 1958.

Jespersen, Otto, *Language, its Nature, Development and Origin.* London: Allen and Unwin, 1922.

Joos, Martin, *Readings in Linguistics: the development of descriptive linguistics in America since 1925.* New York: American Council of Learned Societies, 1958.

Kelly, Leo L., "Dialogue vs Structure," *The French Review,* Vol. XXXVII, No. 4 (February, 1964), pp. 432–439.

Lenard, Yvone, *Jeunes Voix, Jeunes Visages.* New York: Harper & Row, 1970.

——————, *Teacher's Edition of Jeunes Voix, Jeunes Visages.* New York: Harper & Row, 1970.

——————, *Parole et Pensée.* New York: Harper & Row, 1965.

——————, *Parole et Pensée du Professeur.* New York: Harper & Row, 1965.

Lenneberg, Eric H., *Biological Foundations of Language.* New York: John Wiley & Sons, Inc., 1967.

Miller, George A., "The Psycholinguists," *Encounter* 23:1, 1964, pp. 29–37. Reprinted in *Psycholinguistics*, Charles E. Osgood and Thomas A. Sebeok, eds. Bloomington: Indiana University Press, 1965.

Moulton, William G., "Linguistics and Language Teaching in the United States 1940–1960," *Trends in European and American Linguistics 1930–1960*. Christine Mohrmann *et al.*, eds. Utrecht: Spectrum, 1961.

O'Connor, Patricia, and W. F. Twaddell, "Intensive Training for an Oral Approach in Language Teaching." *Modern Language Journal*, Vol. XLIV, No. 2, 1960.

O'Neil, Wayne A., "The Reality of Grammars: Some Literary Evidence." Paper presented to the Linguistic Circle of New York, 1966.

Palmer, Harold E., *One Hundred Substitution Tables*. Cambridge: W. Heffer and Sons Ltd., 1916.

———————————, *The Scientific Study and Teaching of Languages*. New York: World Book Co., 1917.

Penfield, Wilder, "A Consideration of the Neurophysiological Mechanism of Speech and some Educational Consequences," *Proceedings of the American Academy of Arts and Sciences* 82, 1953, pp. 201–214.

Reinert, Harry, *Bulletin of the National Association of Secondary School Principals*. Washington, 1966.

Richards, I. A., "The Secret of 'Feedforward,'" *Saturday Review* (February 3), 1968.

Rutherford, William E., *Modern English*. New York: Harcourt, Brace, & World, Inc., 1968.

Salas, Manual, Paper read to the Foreign Language Teachers Association of the State of Arizona, November, 1959.

Sapir, Edward, "The Psychological Reality of Phonemes" (1933), *The Selected Writings of Edward Sapir*, D. Mandelbaum, ed. Berkeley: University of California Press, 1949.

Sauveur, Lambert, *Introduction to the Teaching of Living Languages without Grammar or Dictionary*. New York: F. W. Christern, 1875.

Scheffler, Israel, *Conditions of Knowledge*. Chicago: Scott, Foresman, and Co., 1965.

Slate Supplement to the General Catalogue. Berkeley: Associated Students of the University of California, Winter, Summer, Fall, 1967.

Smith, Philip, "Static in the Language Lab," *Today's Education*, Vol. 58, No. 7 (October 1969), pp. 49–51.

Stanford, *Academic Standing of Stanford Undergraduates:* April, 1968.

Twaddell, W. Freeman, *On Defining the Phoneme*. Language Monograph No. 16, 1935. Reprinted in Joos, 1958.

——————————————, "Meaning, Habits, and Rules," *Education* 49, 1948.

Weir, Ruth, *Language in the Crib*. The Hague: Mouton, 1961.